# The Wolves Within

An old Cherokee is teaching his grandson about life. "A fight is going on inside me," he said to the boy.

"It is a terrible fight and it is between two wolves. One is evil - he is anger, envy, sorrow, regret, greed, arrogance, self-pity, guilt, resentment, inferiority, lies, false pride, superiority, and ego." He continued, "The other is good - he is joy, peace, love, hope, serenity, humility, kindness, benevolence, empathy, generosity, truth, compassion, and faith. The same fight is going on inside you - and inside every other person, too."

The grandson thought about it for a minute and then asked his grandfather, "Which wolf will win?"

The old Cherokee simply replied, "The one you feed."

# Cognitive Recovery

an empirical program to
promote and sustain recovery from addiction.

First published 2009
Copyright © Steven Salter 2010

# Table of Contents

1       Forward
4       About Addicts
10      The What and Why of CR
14      The Why of Addiction
20      Addiction Disease Concept
23      Transtheoretical Model of Change
26      Am I An Addict?
31      It's All In Your Mind
36      How To Get Clean
41      Staying Clean and Sober
47      Accept That Your Are Addicted
50      Housecleaning/Housekeeping
57      Working With Others
60      Commitment
61      Cognitive Behavioral Therapy
67      Stinking Thinking
71      Dialectic Behavioral Therapy
72      Rational Emotive Behavioral Therapy (REBT)
74      Living Mindfully
80      Living Sober
90      Spirituality and Religion
93      Observing Your Thoughts
97      Meditation
104     Electronic Meditation
106     Relaxation Techniques
108     Closing Thoughts

109     **Appendices**

        Recovery Groups
        CR Meeting Format
        Meetings, Mentors, Therapy
        Worksheets
        Affirmations
        Literature / Sites

# Forward

*One of every eight Americans has a significant problem with alcohol or drugs, with 40 percent of the group having a "dual diagnosis", or concurrent mental/nervous disorder;*

*By age eighteen, almost 12 percent of all young people are illicit drug users;*

*An untreated alcoholic's medical costs are approximately 300 percent higher than non-alcoholic's medical costs;*

*Approximately 70 percent of illegal drug users are employed and contribute significantly to workplace absenteeism, accidents and injuries, decreased productivity, increased insurance expenses, employee turnover costs and on-the-job violence;*

*The estimated annual direct cost to our society resulting from substance abuse is more than 250 billion dollars;*

*It is generally accepted that chemical dependency, along with associated mental health disorders, has become one of the most severe health and social problems facing the United States.*

*Source: SAMHSA (U.S. Substance Abuse and Mental Health Services Administration)*

These are just statistics and while very alarming, are undoubtedly low because it is impossible to know how many people are really addicted. Yes, it is worse, the numbers are much higher. How many people are undiagnosed, misdiagnosed, or ignored? Some researchers estimate that the percentage of the U.S. population who can be classified as addicts (alcohol and other drugs) has risen from 5% to nearly 10% over the past few decades. Addiction on a global scale has continued to grow.

Addiction is a disease of epidemic proportions. It is not going to stop and there is no certain cure. The most popular treatment of addiction since the 1930s has been 12-step programs. However, the recovery rate for 12-step programs has been roughly estimated by some to be approximately 3% to 5% which is about the same as spontaneous remission which is someone just getting sick and tired enough to stop on their own.

There are other methods of recovery including secular recovery groups, pure therapeutic approaches, and new medications. But, addiction recovery groups outside of 12-step oriented ones are not widespread and every day more addicts die, they hurt or kill other people in traffic accidents or through a criminal assault, they suffer horror, guilt, and terror of their own making.

It is clear that more needs to be done. The statistics above do not reflect the human anguish that addiction causes. Billions of people are affected by addiction worldwide. Not just the ones that have an addiction, but their families, friends, and in the case of drunk driving or criminal behaviors, the victims and their families and friends.

Addiction is also still a stigma for the sufferer, even in this day. Addicts are not treated the same as those who suffer from other diseases. Yes, addiction is a disease by the common definition of disease which is "... a condition of the living animal or plant body or of one of its parts that impairs normal functioning and is typically manifested by distinguishing signs and symptoms."

Addiction can clearly be defined then as a mental illness with a physical component. Addiction is a psychobiological disease. You do not have to abandon your intelligence, integrity, religious beliefs (or lack thereof!) to recover from addiction. You can achieve sobriety through an evidence based, cognitive program. However, when I use the word cognitive, I am not saying you can think your way out of addiction.

You cannot think your way out of this problem because the problem is your mind. Certainly there is a biological component to addiction but primarily it is our thoughts, or rather the generated thoughts of our addictive self, that is the real addiction.

Behavioral scientists, therapists, and clinicians support the transtheoretical model of behavioral change. This model defines six distinct stages: precontemplation, contemplation, preparation, action, maintenance, and termination.

When applied to addiction the sixth stage, termination, is generally referred to as "regression" or "relapse". We will talk more about this model of change and how it applies to addiction in another chapter.

It is generally considered that once you are addicted, you will always be, especially in regards to substance abuse. Behaviors can change, habits broken and reprogrammed, but some substances seem to "hard-wire" conditioned responses to our physical bodies. In these cases, abstinence is the only answer. Abstinence and a behavioral change can free one from addiction and addictive behavior.

One key concept in CR is re-programming the conditioned responses you set in place during the time you were using. These conditioned responses include how you react to substances, how you react to external events, and so on.

In this book we will examine addiction, treatment of addiction, and how to recover from addictive behavior. Recovery does indeed happen and millions of people lead totally normal and happy lives afterwards.

This book talks about a human approach to addiction recovery. CR is a program for people. Please notice the plural form of the word. We generally cannot recover alone but must help and learn from others. Social integration is a vital part of recovery. We have deceived ourselves for too long and developed a selfish, self-denying state of withdrawal. The social interaction helps to remove us from a self centered perspective, the one that our inner addict strives to hold onto. Addiction thrives in the secret, dark rooms of your mind. By opening yourself to others honestly you also open the self-locked doors of your mind and illuminate your real Self.

Throughout the book we will use the term "addict" as meaning "one who has the disease of addiction". In CR you do not have to label yourself an alcoholic, addict, or anything at all. You have a disease, that is all.

If you are addicted, read this book, practice the techniques, work with others, and learn to live mindfully you will not only achieve sobriety but you will stay sober and you will find new happiness, serenity, and joy in living.

# About Addicts

*Knowing yourself is the beginning of all wisdom.*
*- Aristotle*

An addict is like anyone else in the world for the most part. The only difference is the mental/physical quirk that makes them an addict. You'll find addicts at every level of society, in every industry, in every community. Addiction does not respect age, wealth, status, or popularity. The wealthiest individuals can be just as addicted as the poorest homeless person. The shining star of Hollywood can be just as addicted as a nondescript citizen of a small town that no one will ever hear of. Addicts can be found in any profession. Judges and doctors, plumbers and electricians, teachers and athletes. You will find pre-teen addicts and septuagenarian addicts. Addiction is a most democratic disease that treats everyone equally.

Some of the brightest individuals and the hardest workers are addicted to something, whether it is a substance or a behavior. At some point, no addict truly enjoys or wants to abuse a substance or act out but they are driven to it by the addictive nature of their disease. Most make solemn vows to never drink again, never smoke again, never gamble again, never cheat on the spouse again, but they end up doing it over and over. They castigate themselves and as time goes by, they begin to hate themselves and regard themselves as failures.

A percentage of addicts end up in trouble with the law. Some manage to accomplish this early on at the start of their addiction and others may take years or decades to reach a point in their active disease phase where they do something obvious enough to run afoul of the law. Why does it take so long sometimes? Some people just "luck out" and miss getting picked up or detected until their luck runs out. Others just have more success at controlling their behavior until the progressive nature of the disease has reached a point where it causes them to do things they never would have before.

Those that do not learn to put the disease of addiction into remission generally lead sad, desperate lives until they die. During their short span on the planet they ruin other lives as well as their own, they create hardship and misery for all who know them. They hate themselves and turn that hate outward to the

4

rest of the world.

However, those that learn to put their disease into remission are some of the most productive, energetic, compassionate, and loving people you will ever meet. This book is all about putting the disease of addiction into lifelong remission.

Consider the average active addict. This individual is a perfect example of someone completely out of control who is desperately trying to achieve some control in their life. The active addict knows in the deepest recesses of their mind that they are unable to control their use of alcohol or another drug, of food, or gambling, whatever it is they are addicted to. They are often bright, highly motivated people who can excel in so many areas of life but are reduced to slavery because of their addiction.

They try to maintain a style of life that they think is normal but they are always driven back to their active addiction. The horror, guilt, shame, and anger of this inability to control will pervade their mind every moment of their life, waking or sleeping. All those emotions can be simply reduced to fear with a capital F. Fear of what will happen, fear of what they will do, fear of financial instability, fear of social gaffes, fear of legal ramifications, fear, fear, fear.

What is the easiest way to escape this fear, at least temporarily? By using again, of course. Alcohol and other drugs can blur the biting edges of reality and allow one to forget the fear for awhile. But using the very substance that caused the fear only creates more fear and strengthens the Beast of addiction.

Every human seems to have an built in urge to control or master their environment. All humans also have aspects to their behavior that may not be quite exemplary or socially acceptable. We addicts have all the "flaws" of human character that everyone else does with the addition of this other deadly component that drives us to lengths many non-addicts would not dream of.

Because we cannot master our addiction, we strive for control in relationships, in business endeavors, in social gatherings, in every aspect of human life. We are driven people, filled with fear and an overwhelming drive to escape it. As our addiction progresses we may give up and seek to escape life altogether, we might shun our former lives and find our standards dropping less and less, we may abandon family, friends, or jobs because we cannot manage our addiction and we helplessly choose our addiction over all else.

We may be filled with false pride and exalt our smallest successes while scorning others. We may whine at the unfairness of life and exclaim, "If only I had a decent break." We may allow anger to fill us and strike back at others, committing crimes and atrocities. We may become deeply depressed and use our substance of choice to blur each day into oblivion. Ah, oblivion is what we seek for we do not have to face ourselves or others when we are blurred from reality.

If we examine our lives and behavior we find no humility, no real tenderness or compassion, no commitment, no acceptance of life whatsoever. It is as if we are living a nightmare we cannot wake from. Regardless of who the addict is, whether presiding on executive boards, scrabbling out a homeless life in filthy city alleys, moving in glittering circles in the entertainment industry, delivering mail, the factory worker, the housewife, the movie star, the clerk, the secretary...the addict hates the slavery they find themselves in and wants to be free.

We examine our life, if we dare, and find it repugnant. We may rationalize and minimize or block out the things we don't want to see but that is just a conscious appraisal. Inside we are full of fear and loathing, inside we find desperation and loneliness, inside we weep in despair no matter how tough or nonchalant an exterior we may present to the world.

The addict is out of control, striving for control because they have absolutely none in part of their lives. But trying to control life is an impossible task, a gauzy dream that one may fantasize about and can never happen. The more we try to control, the more we are proven incapable of it. The vicious spiral of active addiction, attempting to control life, and back to active addiction will eventually end in insanity or death if we do not find a way out.

The addict will often change geographical locations, moving from place to place in an attempt to change the environment enough to escape their addiction. They will change jobs frequently, find new friends, do whatever they can think of to change their lives. The addict will invest heavily into religion or other metaphysical concepts, work with hypnosis and meditation. Typical alcoholics switch from liquor to beer or wine, will try to restrict drinking to specific hours of the day, and will structure their lives around their drinking. They will switch from heroin to cocaine, cocaine to marijuana, switch to pills, to alcohol, and back again.

An addict will seemingly find a solution but incomprehensibly find themselves drinking and drugging again. They make solemn vows but somehow reach a point where they lose all rational thought. They may remember the last relapse and how terrible it was but it is as if they are viewing it through a mist that deadens the pain. They somehow convince themselves that it won't happen this time ... it might not happen this time ... if it does happen so what! They reach a point of no return, a point of "who cares", and they use again. Part of their mind is screaming to not do it but the disease is in control now.

It is incredible to see what an addict will go through and still keep on drinking or drugging. They may be involved in car accidents, spend time in jail, and lose spouses, jobs, families, wealth, and health. But they keep on using!

Consider the insanity of a person who drives a vehicle while impaired. A few tokes of pot, a couple of drinks, a line of coke, whatever the poison is and they are driving impaired and the inner addict rationalizes and bolsters a sick self-ego into thinking they will be ok, that nothing bad will happen to them.

But, it only takes a second of time for a child to chase a ball out into the road in front of you, a car to pull out in front, for your front wheels to drift across the center line, or slip sideways on a slick curve. When you are impaired, that second of time is lost and anything can happen.

Addicts tell themselves it won't happen to them but it does, every single day.

Want more statistics? According to MADD (Mother's Against Drunk Driving),

*On average someone is killed by a drunk driver every 45 minutes. In 2008, an estimated 11,773 people died in drunk driving related crashes—a decline of 9.8 percent from the 13,041 drunk driving related fatalities of 2007.*

*About three in every ten Americans will be involved in an alcohol-related crash at some time in their lives.*

*Fifty to 75 percent of drunk drivers whose licenses are suspended continue to drive!*

*In 2002, surveys estimates that Americans took over 159 million alcohol-impaired driving trips, compared with only 116 million in 1997.*

*Over 1.46 million drivers were arrested in 2006 for driving under the influence of alcohol or narcotics. This is an arrest rate of 1 for every 139 licensed drivers in the United States.*

*A first time drunk driving offender on average has driven drunk 87 times prior to being arrested.*

*Alcohol-related crashes in the United States cost the public an estimated $114.3 billion in 2000, including $51.1 billion in monetary costs and an estimated $63.2 billion in quality of life losses. People other than the drinking driver paid $71.6 billion of the alcohol-related crash bill, which is 63 percent of the total cost of these crashes.*

Most addicts know of these statistics but time after time you hear about the person who was picked up for drunk driving, lost their license, and was picked up the next day driving impaired on a suspended license. What rational person does that sort of thing?

What about the addict that meets their probation officer, or shows up at a Victim Impact Panel, with alcohol on their breath? No person in their right mind would do such an crazy thing. That is the key word, crazy. Addiction most closely resembles a form of insanity than anything else.

The addict expends enormous energy and resources fighting their addiction and fighting life itself. They will become egotistical and opinionated, angry or withdrawn, exhibit behavioral traits they never expressed before. All of this in an effort to break free, to fight the good fight.

But the fight isn't a good fight and they are destined to lose. No matter how strong, how resourceful, how intelligent, or how persistent they are, they are doomed to use again as long as they fight the addiction.

The answer they've been searching for is quite simple; all they have to do is stop fighting. Stop fighting the addiction and stop fighting life. That is what Cognitive Recovery is about, learning to accept life, learning humility, compassion, and honesty. Finding strengths that the addict is completely unaware of.

# The What and Why of CR

*What progress, you ask, have I made? I have begun to be a friend to myself.*
*- Hecato, Greek philosopher*

CR is short for **C**ognitive **R**ecovery. It is a program of addiction recovery. Note that we do not use a plural form for addiction. Terms such as "cross addictions" or "multiple addictions" aren't useful because it is the same mechanism regardless of the substance or behavior. This book will mention alcoholism more often than naught because that drug is the most readily available and socially acceptable one. But one can simply replace the word alcohol with your own drug of choice, whether it be another substance or even a behavior, and everything here will apply. We'll also use the word "addict" to reflect our focus on the disease of addiction rather than a single substance.

There are many recovery programs in existence. 12-Step programs such as AA and NA, LifeRing, S.O.S., S.M.A.R.T., Women for Sobriety, Rational Recovery, and others. Why another program? CR is a partial synthesis of the wisdom, research, and techniques from other recovery methods as well as solid, research based therapeutic techniques and provides a simple, workable solution that anyone can use. CR is a highly flexible, customizable program of recovery. There is no one right way to work on your recovery in CR. We do not insist you adopt a specific belief structure or follow carefully delineated steps of recovery. We offer suggestions that we found worked for us and will certainly work for you.

We offer tools for you to use to create your own toolbox. We realize that no program will work for all and trying to force individuals into a rigid structure will only create havoc. Some recovery programs blame the individual for not following their simple steps but it isn't the individual that is the problem, it is any program that tries to fit all infinitely variable individuals into a single rigid program.

Addicts are generally strong individualists and while this can be a serious drawback in some ways it can also be their salvation. An addict who has the will to live and change can do it. But, if you try to force them into a predefined mold that someone else thinks they should fit into, it usually causes conflicts and other problems.

In CR you use what works for you. We offer suggestions that have worked for us but recognize that not all our suggestions may work for you. Yes, you can get sober and stay sober in CR but you will have to work for it and you will need to WANT it.

We call CR an empirical, evidence based system because we utilize, in part, proven evidence based cognitive therapeutic methods such as CBT (cognitive behavioral therapy) and REBT (rational emotive behavioral therapy. We draw on the accumulated research data that those therapeutic approaches have provided through multitudes of case studies. CR leverages the current research on addiction as well as modern psychotherapeutic techniques to help gain and keep sobriety.

Additionally and perhaps more importantly, we embrace the concepts of acceptance, social integration, and mindfulness to provide a complete model of living in recovery.

Alternative methods are not widespread at this point in time so most likely you won't have a meeting in your locale. In most places, 12-step meetings are the only game in town. This is changing though. Thousands of people have found serenity and happiness in their recovery using alternate programs and that number is increasing daily.

You can always start a meeting! Be the one that cares enough to help others by starting your own secular recovery group in your town. How to do that? The appendix of this book contains information about starting up your own CR meeting. Find like minded people, find a place to hold a meeting, and get started! It is through interaction with others that we find our way to staying clean and sober.

CR is a powerful approach to an abstinence focused lifestyle for addicts. It involves stopping usage of your poison, staying clean, recovering from psychological defense mechanisms you may have developed during your using career, investigating and finding out who you really are under all those layers, and learning how unique, wonderful, and worthy you are.

With CR you are free to utilize just about anything that helps you get well. **Higher powers are optional in CR.** That means that you are encouraged to use your specific religious beliefs if it helps you but we do not believe that recovery from addiction requires a belief in a higher power or god(s).

CR does not believe that addicts are seriously flawed, powerless human beings. We believe that the flaws that some programs talk about are merely the human condition and addicts will often magnify or wallow in those behaviors, usually to a point of excess. But excess seems to be the rule for an addict, is it not? We believe in empowering the individual to recognize, accept, and overcome their problems. We provide common sense methods and exercises to recover through observation, recognition, and acceptance.

CR is a flexible program. You create your own program based on a common set of tools. The one thing that is required is abstinence. If you think you can control your addiction, you are only fooling yourself. You will not read this book and suddenly be surrounded by a white light and a divine knowledge that you are now free. You will need to read the book, talk to others, practice what you have learned, continue to learn, and spend a long time letting go of old behaviors. This is a process, not a magical cure.

The Sobriety Priority is **Don't Use No Matter What!** This means we do whatever it takes to stay clean and sober. If we do not use, we are doing something worthwhile and will have the energy and ability to enjoy and improve our lives. There is never an excuse to use, to allow the inner addict to emerge again.

It is much simpler to remain abstinent than to try to control how much we use. Being abstinent, we don't have to think about when we get our next fix, when we can have a drink, how much money we can afford to spend on our drug of choice, or worry about the number of sick days we have left at work. When we remain abstinent; life is so much simpler, cleaner, and brighter.

CR doesn't focus on negativity, it focuses on empowering the individual, educating the individual, and showing the individual how to detect addictive thoughts and behaviors and release them. CR will help you learn to think differently.

We may talk about CBT/REBT techniques, but you are not expected to practice each therapeutic method exactly or become an expert in any method. CR is all about taking what you need to get and stay sober from these and other systems. What we do with the modern cognitive therapeutic practices is adopt practices and ways of thinking, ways of living that will keep us sober. In addition to these we embrace mindfulness, a concept that has been around as long as humans have been.

After learning to watch your thoughts, really being aware of your thinking, you can learn to change the way you think, which will change the way you feel, which will change the way you behave and perceive life.

Eventually, you will not miss drinking or drugging. What little enjoyment you may have ever gotten from those activities will fade into insignificance compared to the happy, fulfilling life you can have.

It can be a long road but this program is a simple thing to do if you apply yourself to it. How badly do you want sobriety? That will determine your success.

# The Why of Addiction

*We are still masters of our fate.*
*We are still captains of our souls.*
*- Winston Churchill*

The term addiction is used in many contexts to describe an obsession, compulsion, or excessive psychological dependence such as: drug addiction (e.g. alcoholism), video game addiction, crime, money, work addiction, compulsive overeating, problem gambling, computer addiction, nicotine addiction, pornography addiction, plastic surgery addiction, etc. In traditional medical terminology, an addiction is a state in which the body depends on a substance for normal functioning and may occur along with physical dependence. When the drug or substance on which someone is dependent is suddenly removed, it will cause physical/emotional/mental withdrawal, which is observed as a characteristic set of signs and symptoms.

However, the common usage for the term addiction has grown to include psychological dependence. In this context, the term is used in drug addiction and substance abuse problems, but also refers to behaviors that were not traditionally recognized by the medical community as addictive problems, such as compulsive overeating, gambling, sexual behavior, and so on. These recurring compulsions to engage in some specific activity, despite harmful consequences, are clearly psychological addictions.

## The biology of addiction

The physical mechanism of addiction has been understood for decades. It all revolves around the reward centers of our brain. As humans evolved, our brains developed a "feel-good" mechanism to reward activities or behaviors that promoted self and species survival. Thus, activities such as eating, finding a warm place to sleep, engaging in sexual intercourse, and a host of other things actually create a reward response in us. We just feel good when we do certain things. Of course, in modern societies this generic reward response can be triggered from many activities far removed from the simple species survival.

Addiction happens when a substance or activity becomes identified by our subconscious as a survival type mechanism worthy of hooking into our reward centers. Alternately, an activity that gives us pleasure can be mistakenly identified by our minds as a survival type mechanism because of the reward we initially get when we do it.

Why this happens, no one really knows for certain yet but the result is that a person will be subconsciously driven to abuse a drug or behavior much in the same way as we are driven to eat, sleep, and procreate.

Addiction is not just a bad habit. You can eradicate bad habits through different methods but addiction seems to originate from the deep, limbic layers of our brains that support involuntary responses.

Researchers have mapped out the biology of addiction through extensive study and analysis. The reward circuit includes the ventral tegmental area, VTA, which is connected to the nucleus accumbens and the prefrontal cortex in the pathway where they communicate through various neuronal pathways. The ventral striatum is a major component in this system and is usually considered to be the part of the striatum that is associated with limbic structures, such as the amygdala, hippocampus, midline thalamus, and various regions of the prefrontal cortex. The ventral striatum is also strongly innervated by dopaminergic fibers from the VTA and has a high density of serotonergic inputs. Serotonin is a neurotransmitter that helps regulate behavior such as appetite and emotions.

The natural function of the reward circuitry is to provide a pleasurable feeling in response to functions that sustain our lives, such as eating or reproductive activities. This reward encourages us to repeat such activities. Imagine how powerful such behaviors are. They are survival instincts that are programmed into us at an almost cellular level.

The reward circuitry functions through the use of chemical neurotransmitters such as dopamine. When the circuit is activated it will trigger the release of dopamine, which creates the "feel good" response. Drugs stimulate this same response, sometimes to a greater degree than the natural responses intended by the evolutionary creation of reward centers, causing a larger spike in dopamine levels. The immediate reward that drugs give us can cause us to bypass other activities and we eventually condition ourselves to a specific substance because our reward circuitry requires it now.

Addiction comes about from changes resulting in the brain due to a large dosage or frequent long-term use. Since the natural level of dopamine is now artificially elevated, a need for more stimulation is required. A perfect example is nicotine addiction. Non-smokers don't need the nicotine boost every hour or so but the nicotine addict feels driven to smoke to restore an unnaturally elevated level. Nicotine, as a drug, certainly does not relax the smoker but it does elevate dopamine and nicotine levels that mimic a relaxed state. Any cocaine or heroin addict knows the exact same feeling.

Circuits altered in the brain will change the way the neurons in the system work. All these changes can be either short term or long term. The behavior of the person as well as the behavior of the brain is influenced by a physical change. Thus, drug addiction can be considered a pathological subversion of normal brain processes. This subversion is reinforced by drug induced stimuli and compulsive behavior will result.

That is the technical description. A simple analogy can suffice for most purposes though. Consider an activity such as drinking as if you were dragging a nail along a soft surface. You leave a shallow groove in the surface the first time you do it. If you repeat this, the groove gets deeper. In the initial stages, you can stop the activity by slipping out of the groove, but as time goes on, the groove gets so deep that it is difficult to get over the side of the groove. You usually just follow it to the end, regardless of whether or not you had planned to. Eventually, it seems as if you are powerless to stop the activity once you have started. Everytime you start, you slide into the well worn groove and the groove is now a chasm.

A certain percentage of the human population appears to become easily addicted to substances and behaviors. They appear to possess a genetically transmitted propensity for this since studies show that addictive behavior seems to run in specific families. It is common to examine an addict's familial history and discover parents, grandparents, and other relatives with the same problem. However, as stated above, addiction can occur simply through long-term use or a high dosage.

16

Note a bit of hope here for those addicts who are young and do not have a lot of years of active addiction behind them. The neurological changes in the brain can be short term or long term. The quicker you start recovery, the better off you are. You generally have less damage to recover from and have less physiological changes to your brain. I've known several teenagers or people in their early 20's who somehow just accepted their disease completely and have a much easier time recovering. The toughest part for them is dealing with peer pressure. Of course, that is a problem for all of us, is it not?

## The reality of addiction

Addiction is such a powerful thing because it is associated with the deepest, most primal urges of our biology. We are all driven by these urges to maintain life. We need to breathe, to eat, to sleep. If we do not do these things then we die.

Since addicts have conditioned themselves to react to substances or behaviors as if they were survival actions, they find themselves almost helpless to resist the siren call of addiction. The addictive voice is their own and it knows the addict as well as they know themself.

 Our reward centers now react differently from non-addicts and we have powerful mental compulsions that reduce our ability to control our usage of substances. How easy it is to regard using again as a form of insanity when we already know what is going to happen. But, we will do it over and over, vainly hoping that this time it will be different. The results will not be much different because we have programmed ourselves to react in specific ways now.

We talk ourselves into hoping vainly that there will be a different outcome. The addict in us wants to use and doesn't care about health or society. The addict in us doesn't care about our bodies, or minds, or other people. The addict in us is a mental construct we created at some point in time that only cares about using. It is strengthened and supported by the physiological changes that were created during the addictive process.

As described earlier, addiction is a low level mental dysfunction originating in the meso-limbic reward centers that often substitutes or overrides basic instincts such as eating,

17

procreation, and other survival activities. Being such a low level function, it is not easily overcome since it has hooks into the behaviors that drive us to sustain existence.

The addictive self is almost like another being inhabiting your body. It is ironic that, being a product of hijacked reward centers that deal with basic survival mechanisms, it cares nothing for survival but is focused completely on instant gratification, on oblivion, on raw hedonistic pleasures. An addict will go without nutrition, without meaningful social contact, or without basic personal hygiene during their reckless plunge in active addiction.

This addictive self lives on the subconscious level and works to influence your conscious decisions. The more energy it gets, the more it manifests on the conscious level. If left to itself, it insinuates the influence into every part of your life, into every emotion, belief, and value system.

We will refer to this as the "addictive self" or "the Beast" in the book, for this part of you is completely unlike the rest of you. It cares for nothing but using and what it regards as pleasure. Nothing is enough for it and if you manage to sate it temporarily, it will only want more in a very short time. It cannot have enough food, enough alcohol, enough sex, enough nicotine or caffeine, enough anger, anxiety, or enough depression.

The term "Beast" can express a personification of this disease quite nicely but feel free to use any term you like: Demon, Beast, Disease, Addictive Self, Little Monster, or whatever. Just remember that this is not separate from you but a psychological malady that stems from your subconscious self and is driven by a biological origin.

The Beast thrives on negative emotions because through those emotions it knows you will drink/drug/act out again no matter how much you really don't want to. The Beast can be considered an insane component of your own self that works tirelessly to bring you to the same state. However, the Beast will cheerfully utilize positive emotions and exaggerate them to fool you into using again.

How to fight such a thing? No wonder some recovery programs talk about "demon rum" and adherents throw themselves to their knees, pleading with their gods for assistance. How else can you fight a demon but through divine intervention? If we were talking about demons I'd be all for gods, crucifixes, holy water, and silver bullets but this is no demon, this is a psychobiological disease. Fighting it just feeds it. What we need to do is accept that it exists and then let it fade away into impotence.

The Beast is compulsive and will try to affect all aspects of your life. That is why so many people are addicted to more than one thing. It isn't the substance or behavior; it is the addictive self inside you. The Beast, once activated, is so powerful that people will choose their substance of choice over loved ones, food, or shelter.

But, the Beast is no demon, no mystical entity at all, just part of you that is sick, mis-programmed. The way to fight the Beast is by not fighting. Every time you try to fight it, you just feed it more energy. By recognizing it, by observing and dismissing the Beast, you gain power where you could not have power before. By focusing on positives instead of negatives, you ascend from the dark, mouldering depths of your Beastly self into a light of hope, happiness, and tranquility.

You do this and no one can do it for you. But, other people are essential to the process. The Beast loves isolation because it works in solitude and secrecy. So many addicts are shocked when they relapse. But, if they look back, they can see how they slowly were sliding away from sobriety, a tiny bit at a time. The Beast is subtle and cunning and few can gain freedom from their addiction without the help of others, because other people are our mirrors. They reflect what we often cannot see in ourselves. By focusing on other people, we remove the selfish focus from ourselves. This is one of the best ways to achieve detachment from the Beast.

As Winston Churchill said, "We are still masters of our fate...". We do not have to give up, to surrender to this disease, to become hopeless and resigned, to be a slave to our Beast. We know for an absolute certainty that anyone can put the disease into remission and in the process become a much happier, healthier, more productive individual.

# Addiction Disease Concept

*If we all did the things we are capable of,*
*we would astound ourselves.*
*- Thomas Edison*

Some people object to the disease concept of addiction, but consider the common definition of the word disease:

"...a condition of the living animal or plant body or of one of its parts that impairs normal functioning and is typically manifested by distinguishing signs and symptoms."

Addiction fits this definition perfectly. Consider the alcoholic who struggles to control his drinking and behavior. If the alcoholic was functioning normally, there would be no struggle. This is the same with any substance abuse including nicotine, caffeine, and so on. Consider the gambler who is hooked on beating the odds, continually losing money at casinos or on-line games. This is not normal functioning as all. Follow this concept through for the sex addict, the shopper who always has to buy something to feel good, and the person who craves the excitement of stealing.

As mentioned earlier, addiction is a psychobiological disease that has components in our biology and psychology. It is a complex, interwoven structure that we do not fully understand. We may not be able to cure this right now but we can learn to live with it and not succumb to addictive impulses.

Addicts have suffered neurological changes in their brain and nervous system. The disorder manifests in long term obsessive-compulsive behaviors. Addictions are often based in physical dependency created by altered neurotransmitter balances and driven by new neurological pathways which have been established to sustain the condition. The new neurological pathways are permanently established, and they will not simply disappear.

There is no magic pill or therapy to fix this. Science may come up with a way someday to apply a combined biological and psychological treatment to rectify this condition but it still is not totally understood. The longer you stay an active addict though, the harder it is to recover since you continue to create more neurological pathways and reinforce addictive behaviors the longer you use. There is no other human malady that encompasses the psychological and biological the way the disease of addiction does.

The primary neurological disorder is only complicated by physical dependence on the substances. The physical dependence on the substances is a secondary result. Physical drug withdrawal does not remove the underlying neurological/behavioral addictive disorder.

Distinguishing signs and symptoms are profuse. Some obvious signs that most addicts share are:
- Overt mood changes – happy, sad, excited, anxious, and so on.
- Changes in energy – extremely tired or energetic with no apparent reason.
- Secretiveness, isolation, lying.
- Stealing and unpredictable finances.
- Unexpected illness.

Most of us have seen those behaviors in ourselves or others. The addict may think they are covering their tracks but it is usually quite obvious to those close to them.

It is pretty obvious now that addiction can be classified as a disease, especially when you consider the technical description in the previous chapter. Addicts have a problem in their bodies and minds that prevent them from acting "normally".

## How Does Someone Get This Disease?

Addiction appears to be "contracted" in one of two ways. You can inherit the propensity for it or you can just get it by regularly abusing substances or behaviors. Some people seem to almost instantly become addicted to drugs such as alcohol whereas it takes other people a lot of abuse before they are hooked.

There has been a lot of research in the last fifty years concerning addiction and definite familial trends have been found. If a specific individual is an addict, there is often a good chance that siblings, parents, or grandparents exhibit the same behavior. Even siblings separated from birth, raised in different locales will show the same addictive behavior. This certainly implies a genetic factor to addiction.

Another way to become addicted is to just overdo something regularly. There are many cases where individuals will reach young adulthood and start drinking or drugging on a regular basis and at some point, they find they cannot stop. No one else in their genetic background exhibits like behavior but they are definitely addicted.

Addicts tend to engrave pathways of behavior that are hooked into our basic reward systems and are thereafter locked into what appears to be a parasympathetic response to the stimulus that is generated by substances or certain behaviors. Our very natures make it much easier to pick up new habits since we've basically hardwired our subconscious minds to react in these ways. We can overdo almost anything. That is why so many addicts find that moderation in almost anything is nearly impossible. If it feels good, we want a lot of it.

A lot of people want to determine how they became addicted and often blame relatives for an inherited propensity toward addiction, or a life situation that found them abusing a substance. Ask yourself right now, does it really matter why I am addicted? It is a fact now and cannot be changed. The how doesn't matter anymore. What matters is overcoming the addiction and regaining your life.

# Transtheoretical Model of Change

*There's only one corner of the universe you can be certain of improving, and that's your own self.*
*- Aldous Huxley*

As mentioned in the Forward of this book, behavioral scientists and therapists support the transtheoretical model of change, a method of observing and explaining how our behavior changes. A key concept to this model is that behavior changes over time rather than suddenly.

Individual motivation is the most important facet of change and, in fact, a key practice in therapy to helping the individual recognize that they need to change is called Motivational Interviewing. This type of interaction between client and therapist involves open-ended questions, affirmations, reflective listening, and summaries. An experienced therapist can accomplish a great deal and help the client considerably through the application of these methods.

There are six stages to the transtheoretical model of change which include precontemplative, contemplative, preparation, action, maintenance, and regression.

The precontemplative stage is one in which the individual does not recognize there is a problem and does not see a need for change. Traditionally, this was called the Denial stage. All addicts go through this stage and some may remain in it for years or even decades.

The contemplative stage is when the individual becomes aware that there is a problem but isn't sure what to do about it. They may not be certain it is a big problem and they usually think they can just moderate or take care of it themselves. They will often weigh the pros and cons of continuing their behavior.

The preparation stage sees the addict uneasy and feeling they have to do something. They often cut back on usage of the substance or set restrictions on how much and when they use. The addict in this stage may still be a bit uncertain that the problem is as big as might seem and will spend an enormous amount of energy trying to apply self control.

The action stage is where the addict actively works to release the addiction. Bottles will be poured out, all drugs and paraphernalia thrown away, therapy or outpatient services pursued, and recovery meetings attended. The addict is determined to stop acting addictively. After six to twelve months of this action stage the addict is ready to maintain their newly sober lifestyle.

Maintenance is the stage where the addict keeps doing whatever they are doing to stay clean and sober. They often look back at the past with disbelief that they had acted the say they did. Maintenance can be a dangerous stage though because the addict may begin to feel complacent and might begin reaquiring old habits of thinking. They may slack off on meetings and feel they are well or even cured. Don't fall into that trap!

The regression, or relapse, stage occurs when the addict does not keep up with their maintenance program. They find themselves using again. They often will be flooded with emotions of guilt, shame, or anger but those emotions are not useful. If this last stage does occur, the addict should not waste time lamenting their relapse but should immediately get back to the action stage. Continuing to use only causes more damage.

As you look over this transtheoretical model of change, where are you? Do you have a problem at all? Do you have a problem and don't know what to do about it or how serious it is? Have you recognized that you are afflicted with addiction and are working to stay clean and sober? Are you maintaining a clean and sober lifestyle?

It is important to remember that change occurs over time. You might dump the bottle of vodka down the sink but the underlying pre-conditioned reponses are still inside. To release those responses and substitute them with healthy ones will take time.

You have to motivate yourself to change, no one can do it for you although a good therapist practiced in Motivational Interviewing can assist you greatly. Don't feel embarrassed at going to a therapist or worry about the cost. The cost of treatment is miniscule if you compare it to the cost of continuing to use.

Why do you want to change? It seems that most people change because the pain and fear has gotten to a point that they can't manage it any more. They don't want their lives to be the way they are. They want freedom and release.

Examine your own motivations. Discuss your current life and what you would like it to be with someone else. Don't settle for muddling through the world, chained to substances and aberrant behaviors. Reach for the sky and embrace your humanity and freedom.

# Am I An Addict?

*If we are facing in the right direction, all we have to do is keep on walking.*
*-- Buddhist Proverb*

Are you an addict? Do you have a problem with substances or behaviors that create a negative impact on your life? Did you get in trouble with the law because of a substance such as a DUI, public intoxication, possession of a controlled substance, or some other problem? Do you find yourself wanting to drink or use every day?

How has substance use affected your life? It doesn't have to be a substance either! We humans can become addicted to behaviors just as easily. Gambling, pornography, exercise, shopping, or just about anything can be abused.

Think about it. Why are you reading this book? Do you have a problem? Are you addicted to something? If you are unsure, try controlled drinking/using. For alcohol, have two drinks and stop. Better yet, have two drinks, order a third and leave half of it. Don't drink again for several months and do the same thing. Have three or four beers and just stop even though others are still drinking. Can you do that?

Do you always want more? Do you have to control your intake? People who are not addicted don't have a need to control themselves. Addicts always want more.

Here is a simple self-scored test called the Audit Alcohol Addiction test. It is a widespread self-test in common use in the therapeutic community. Take it and be totally, brutally honest with yourself. You don't have to share your answers with anyone else. This is for your benefit. Anywhere you see the word alcohol, please substitute it with your own preferred substance.

## The AUDIT Alcohol Addiction (Alcoholism) Test

To correctly answer some of these questions you need to know the definition of a drink. For this test one drink is:
One can of beer (12 oz or approx 330 ml of 5% alcohol), or
One glass of wine (5 oz or approx 140 ml of 12% alcohol), or
One shot of liquor (1.5 oz or approx 40 ml of 40% alcohol).

**1. How often do you have a drink containing alcohol?**
Never (score 0)
Monthly or Less (score 1)
2-4 times a month (score 2)
2-3 times a week (score 3)
4 or more times a week (score 4)

**2. How many alcoholic drinks do you have on a typical day when you are drinking?**
1 or 2 (0)
3 or 4 (1)
5 or 6 (2)
7-9 (3)
10 or more (4)

**3. How often do you have 6 or more drinks on one occasion?**
Never (0)
Less than monthly (1)
Monthly (2)
Weekly (3)
Daily or almost daily (4)

**4. How often during the past year have you found that you drank more or for a longer time than you intended?**
Never (0)
Less than monthly (1)
Monthly (2)
Weekly (3)
Daily or almost daily (4)

**5. How often during the past year have you failed to do what was normally expected of you because of your drinking?**
Never (0)
Less than monthly (1)
Monthly (2)
Weekly (3)
Daily or almost daily (4)

**6. How often during the past year have you had a drink in the morning to get yourself going after a heavy drinking session?**
Never (0)
Less than monthly (1)
Monthly (2)
Weekly (3)
Daily or almost daily (4)

**7. How often during the past year have you felt guilty or**

**remorseful after drinking?**
Never (0)
Less than monthly (1)
Monthly (2)
Weekly (3)
Daily or almost daily (4)

**8. How often during the past year have you been unable to remember what happened the night before because of your drinking?**
Never (0)
Less than monthly (1)
Monthly (2)
Weekly (3)
Daily or almost daily (4)

**9. Have you or anyone else been injured as a result of your drinking?**
No (0)
Yes, but not in the past year (2)
Yes, during the past year (4)

**10. Has a relative, friend, doctor, or health care worker been concerned about your drinking, or suggested that you cut down?**
No (0)
Yes, but not in the past year (2)
Yes, during the past year (4)

Your score:
If you scored 8-10 or more, you are probably addicted to alcohol.

It may seem like the AUDIT questionnaire is a pretty easy test to fail. If you applied this test to other aspects of your life you undoubtedly could find other areas of addiction. Some people eat too much, fish too much, garden too much, work too much, watch too much television, and so on. Now, those might be addictions but the AUDIT test is highly accurate when focused on alcohol and other drugs.

The AUDIT (Alcohol Use Disorders Identification Test) was developed by the World Health Organization (WHO). The test correctly classifies 95% of people into either alcoholics or non-alcoholics.

**The CAGE Addiction Test**

Here is another simple test is surprisingly accurate. Answer yes or no to each question.

 - Have you ever felt you should <u>C</u>ut down your use of drugs (alcohol or other)?

- Have you ever been <u>A</u>nnoyed when people have commented on your use?

- Have you ever felt <u>G</u>uilty or badly about your use?

- Have you ever used drugs to <u>A</u>void the low feeling you get after using, or to avoid withdrawal symptoms?


Your score:
Score one point for each yes answer.

If you scored 1, there is an 80% chance you're addicted
If you scored 2, there is an 89% chance you're addicted
If you scored 3, there is a 99% chance you're addicted
If you scored 4, there is a 100% chance you're addicted


How did you do? Is there a problem? Are you addicted to alcohol or another drug? Examine your behavior in regards to alcohol and other drugs. Compare that behavior with others. Only you can make the decision that you are an addict.

Not all addicts behave the same although they all have the same disease. Consider the alcoholic that goes on a binge every few months. They don't even think of alcohol until all of a sudden they decide to indulge. They may even make careful plans to set aside the time from work to take days off. Compare those people with the daily drinkers who have to keep a certain level of alcohol in their systems every day.

Even among the daily drinkers are the ones that only drink after work or after a specific time. Then there are the lost ones that wander through life in an alcoholic blur, living from drink to drink. A cocaine user may smoke crack or snort a line only on weekends or they may do it every day. Everyone's specific addictive behavior is different.

Regardless of the frequency or intensity of use, if the addict finds themselves driven to use in spite of their best intentions then it is a problem. Addiction is a progressive disease as well. The longer you stay in active addiction, the more intense it becomes and the more out of control you may find yourself.

The pot smoker who only smokes in the evenings may find themself taking a joint to work so they can go out at lunchtime and catch a buzz. They may try to cut down and make a vow to skip a day or two but when they get home they tell themselves "Oh, it is just pot. What will it hurt?" and take a few tokes....and a few more...and a few more. That is symptomatic of addiction, the need to have more.

It is typical to hear of the alcoholic who switches types of alcohol and limits themselves so they can function. They will try to skip days but there is the irrepressible craving to "just have one". Of course, that always leads to another and another.

Nicotine addicts typically smoke a cigarette approximately once an hour. The level of nicotine has dropped enough that the addictive Beast starts clamoring for another fix in that amount of time. But, how many smokers find themselves chain smoking one after another at times? A hard core smoker will light up when they have pneumonia and can barely breathe. Less dramatic but equally crazy is the smoker who has a bad cold and between coughs and sneezes, puffs on a cigarette. The smoker knows that the harsh, toxic cigarette smoke is only causing more harm, preventing them from healing, but they are driven to continue. A smoker with cancer and on oxygen will remove their oxygen mask to sneak in a few puffs.

Only you can decide if you are an addict. Examine your lifestyle and your relationship with drugs and behaviors. If you find them getting in your way but you still indulge in them, you are probably an addict.

# It's All In Your Mind

*Things do not change; we change.*
*- Henry David Thoreau*

Addiction is baffling to not only ourselves but especially to the non-addicted. How many times have we heard people say "Why do they keep doing it?", "How could they do that to themselves?", and so on. Non-addicts cannot understand the seemingly overwhelming obsession that grips us at times. Don't be surprised, we can't rationally understand it either. An addict might go through months or years of living clean and sober and suddenly relapse back into the horrors of uncontrolled using again. Afterwards (if there IS an afterwards) they'll be astonished, guilty, shocked, and confused. How could it have happened?

It is as if we have two minds, two persons living in the same body. One is the person we think we are, the one living in the world day to day. The other is a non-thinking, amoral creature. The addictive Beast doesn't care about health, finances, the feelings of others, or our personal welfare. It only wants to use.

This Beast is like a parasite that is intertwined with our own minds. It uses our own thoughts and emotions to get what it craves. It will whisper strands of interrelated thoughts into our minds and make us feel sad, depressed, angry, jealous, anything it can to push us off balance. It will take the most irrational thoughts and make them seem reasonable to us.

How to recognize this Beast, this addiction, this disease, this parasite? You can never destroy it. It will always be a part of you, at least until science comes up with a multi-modal treatment to satisfy the biological, mental, and emotional aspects of addiction.

The Beast is part of us and thus knows every button to push. Be aware of negativity in your emotions and thoughts. All humans have periods where they are down or angry but addicts will seize those times and magnify them, wallow in grief, anger, resentment, or self-righteousness.

It is ok to feel irritated that someone cut you off in traffic. It is not ok to think about it over and over until you are trembling with anger and wish the other driver would crash. It is not ok to cut someone else off in traffic to get back at the world. It is not ok to hang onto the irritation. This goes for anything that happens in your life.

Our addictive selves want anger, resentment, despair, hopelessness. Through those negative emotions it can erode our resolve, our rationality, our hope. Through those emotions it can overcome our natural rationality and make the most insane thoughts sound feasible.

This is a struggle with self, or perhaps it is better to phrase it as a struggle with selves. Everyone has what seems to be a dark side but it is especially apparent in addicts. Be wary of your thoughts and your emotions. It is normal and healthy to feel but if negative thoughts and feelings seem to dominate you at times, it is probably the addict in you struggling to get out.

Addiction when you are not actively using is 100% mind. You do not have to listen to the Beast, the addictive self. It is vital to learn how to recognize the addictive voice so you can make the right decisions.

How do you recognize your addictive voice? The first giveaway is any thought or emotion that has to do with using a substance or behavior as you did in the past. Your addictive self IS you, knows every button to push and is incredibly clever at disguising the motive. You may find yourself idly thinking of having a beer on a hot day or a nice glass of wine with dinner. That thought might come more often until it is a constant harangue. You might think that you are an alcoholic and can't drink but others can. You tell yourself that is ok, you don't need the stuff. But, the thought comes back in various forms. You may feel irritated at things, lose patience, and have trouble concentrating. Those are all methods that your Beast is using to wear you down and you may not even realize it!

The best way to resolve such sneaky, underhanded Beastly tricks is to talk to someone. Explain what is going on in your life, in your mind. Just by talking about it you will find yourself realizing what is happening. That is why talking with other people, other recovering addicts, is so important. You can talk to anyone but a fellow addict has been where you have been, felt the same things, done the same things. The fellow addict has a stake in you staying sober and clean. It is true that helping other addicts helps you as well. It is all a part of getting out of your own head, focusing less on yourself than on others.

If you get a thought such as "I want a beer" or "I'd like a nice glass of wine with supper" you need to remember that YOU don't want that drink, it is the addict in you that does. As mentioned in the AVRT technique of Rational Recovery, the addictive self will switch pronouns from "I" to "you" to "we" for anything it can use. All you have to do is remind yourself that it isn't you that wants a drug, it is the addict in you. That can often allow you to regain your balance.

When you are irritable for no apparent reason, low on patience, frustrated easily, find yourself worrying, tending to obsess on things, whatever the behavior is, we often talk about that in CR as "Beastly behavior" or "I'm feeling Beastly today".

That means we are aware that our addictive self is active for some reason. When you recognize that you need to examine your thoughts and emotions. Use the CBT techniques we will talk about in a couple of chapters. Talk with other people. Remind yourself that YOU are absolutely OK at this moment in time. Focus on the immediate moment and take a deep breath. Let it out and smile. You are in charge. That is a basic truth that all addicts must learn. The addictive self, the Beast, can only suggest, can only harass you. It cannot take a drink or other drug or engage in a behavior without you agreeing.

That sounds really simple then, doesn't it? Just say no? Well, in theory it is but our addictive self can literally drive us crazy. After so many subconscious cues, wheedling, misleading, nudges, and outright shoves, our normally rational minds turn irrational. That happens because we aren't aware what is happening before it is too late. The trick is to become aware, avoid negativity, accept life and stay as positive as possible.
It isn't always easy to stay positive. It is easy to say "Just accept life no matter what" but in practice it can be difficult. We get down about things or angry or frustrated. It is ok to feel those things but try not to wallow in them. No matter how much you try to let go, to accept, you sometimes just feel lousy.

Someone with serious financial problems can accept that is how it is and try to focus on the moment. Someone with a court appearance coming up or jail time might accept that is the way it is and just say "Right now, I don't have to worry". Someone in the midst of a failing relationship can just bear with it and be as honest and understanding as possible.

But, we are human and people, places, and things will often affect us. We will feel enraged at corporations or governments, we will fear the trend of society and the darkness or lack of morality we may see. We may be anxious about the future or regret what we did in the past.

Ok then, shout, jump up and down, shake your fist, cry, EXPRESS WHAT YOU FEEL and then take a deep breath and remind yourself that you are who you are and where you are.

The human mind runs almost constantly and that is the biggest problem with being human. An incredible blessing it is to have a rational, expressive, calculating, and imaginative mind but this is also the curse of humanity. Non-addicts are no better off than addicts in this regard and that is rather obvious to see if you consider the emotional and mental aberrations that have flourished throughout history. Consider the power struggles, the focus on material wealth, the utter fascination with famous people, the absolute lack of morality that leaders of businesses and countries so often display. Consider the horrifying wars and crime, the accumulation of wealth, power, or status beyond any sane reason.

Sanity is a tenuous thing at best with so many human beings. We easily get sidetracked from important things, like enjoying life, and waste our time and lives pursuing trivial goals, materialism, power, or fear.

Our inner addict has all that to work with and more. The Beast has only one weapon and that is your own thoughts. How many times do mental dialogs whirl through your head? How often do we imagine faults or slights and find ourselves obsessing on it, getting angrier or more despairing with every cycle of thought?

The Beast will avidly feed any resentment, any anger, or any sadness that you feel. Thoughts will fuel any emotions you have that will, in turn, fuel more negative thoughts. It is a vicious cycle that can be difficult to break out of.

All humans have this mental beast but an addict has a Beast with a capital B. We cannot afford to stay resentful. We cannot afford to stay angry. We must find a balance, a place of non-judgment and acceptance. Let the others wallow in their misery if they like but it will kill us because our addictive selves intensify the cyclical phenomena to the point that our previously conditioned responses lead us back to using again.

Yes, it is all in our minds and if you stay focused on negative things, you are only feeding your Beast. Coping strategies are great to get you out of the negative moment and help you to regain your balance. You can talk to other people and tell them what is going on with you. Just speaking with another person can allow you to let go and relax. You can get busy and do something! Mow the yard, wash the dishes, take your clothes to the laundromat, go for a walk, read a book, just do something. Sitting and mulling over things can just keep you in the doldrums. Do Something!

No one can do this for you and even if you find it difficult at first, anyone and everyone CAN accomplish it. We are not powerless or weak. We may be vulnerable at times and we may make mistakes as all humans do, but we are not mistakes. We can break the cycle, we can accept, we can let go of the thoughts and emotions that afflict us. Now is the time to take charge of your life.

# How To Get Clean and Sober

*Our greatest glory is not in never falling but in rising every time we fall.*
*- Confucius*

CR is a program for you, the individual. You do not have to believe in a god, you do not even have to believe in yourself at first. That will come in time but know that you CAN believe in yourself. You CAN achieve freedom from active addiction. Gradually you will change and you will become stronger and more vital than you have ever been in your life! There is basically one thing you must do and that is to **be abstinent**. Without abstinence, the Beast of your addiction is still in control, still vigorously awake and blurring your perceptions and thoughts.

If you accept that you are an addict or have a problem that might be an addiction then you are heading in the right direction. If you can't even admit to yourself that you have a problem, you will always have that problem. But, if you accept there is a problem or addiction, you have a chance to identify, accept, and overcome it. These are the all important, critical things you must do initially. Admit and Accept.

Just remember, recovery will take time. This involves education, awareness, and change. It also requires patience and time. But it is worth it! You may despair at times of being able to change but if you want this bad enough, you will receive it. Sobriety, serenity, and mindfulness are all there waiting for you to make them your own.

One interesting fact that is worth to mention is that good things happen to addicts that stay sober. There are many reasons for this. A big component of this is that when we get sober and work on improving our selves, we naturally sabotage ourselves less. The addictive self inside always works to sabotage your life. The more stress the Beast can create, the better chance you will relapse. When you put the Beast to sleep, you naturally have less stress.

It also seems that when we are not fighting life, trying to get our own way, that good things just seem to happen. If we are not anxious and in a hurry but open and confident, that open parking place seems to be there, we hit green traffic lights instead of red, and so on. Perhaps by attuning ourselves more to how life itself works rather than struggling against it, we are naturally influencing how it works for us. There are too many stories about good things happening to addicts that don't use to discount this.

**Don't Use, no matter what!**

That is the Sobriety Priority. As long as you do not use, you are ahead of the game. Everything else comes after that one simple priority in life.

If you are having problems not using at all, you need to do some intensive work initially. Attending group therapy, recovery meetings of any type including 12-step meetings, talking with others are all helpful ways to focus on something other than using. The big thing is to stop hiding. You must get out there in the open with other alcoholics/addicts and just accept yourself as you are. When you are around other addicts, you find that you aren't nearly as "bad" as you may have thought you were. That is why I mentioned 12-step meetings. CR may not agree with a lot of 12-step concepts but just being around other addicts can be important.

For alcohol, there are several drugs out there that help to block alcohol from affecting your biochemistry and reduce or eliminate cravings. Please note that CR is not recommending use of these chemicals carte blanche but is offering information for those who might need them. Naltrexone, Ondansotron (Zofran), topiramate, and acamprosate (Campran) all show levels of effectiveness in this regard. For other substance addictions there are other medications, I've only mentioned ones specifically utilized for weaning a person from alcohol. Talk to your doctor to see what might work best for you and your substance of abuse.

By reducing the urge to drink the individual can focus more on behavioral changes and possibly initiate a lifelong recovery much easier than "white knuckling" it. This is really a common sense approach to the cravings problem. However, a good rule of thumb is, the less drugs you take the better off you are. This is not to say that those of us who are under medical supervision or require mood stabilizer drugs should avoid those! Always talk to your doctor before changing any prescribed medication.

If you are struggling not to drink every day then one of these might be a good fit for you. If you only get occasional urges to drink or use, why add another chemical into the mix? Talk it over with other addicts, with an addictions specialist, with your doctor and make a decision. The key thing you want to accomplish is to remain sober.

**Naltrexone** (also known as Trexan®, ReVia®, and Depade®), is very useful because of its action as an Opioid-blocker within the body. If an alcoholic chooses to drink while taking this medication, the euphoric effects of the alcohol would be significantly less than if they were not on this medication. It appears to also effectively block the effects of drugs in the opiate class including heroin, morphine, codeine, and others, and is considered to reduce the craving for both alcohol and opiates. However, this drug is not recommended for patients with liver damage or disease.

**Acamprosate**, also known by the brand name Campral, is a drug used for treating alcohol dependence. Acamprosate is thought to stabilize the chemical balance in the brain that is disrupted by alcoholism. Research indicates that acamprosate works most effectively with a combination of therapy and abstinence from alcohol.

**Ondansetron** might be useful and effective for treating withdrawal symptoms of opioid addictions. Ondansetron lowers the cravings for alcohol, especially in early-onset alcoholics. In one cognitive-behavioral therapy study, ondansetron patients with early-onset alcoholism had fewer drinks per day and more days without drinking anything at all, compared to the other groups in the study.

**Topiramate** is a sulfamate-substituted monosaccharide. Topiramate is quickly absorbed after oral use. Topiramate appears to lessen alcohol cravings and seems capable as a mood stabilizer.

However, those medications can be expensive and if you can't afford them, the only option you have (or prefer) is to just do without your drug of choice. In that case, focus on each day at a time or even each hour at a time. If you are good at procrastination then use that to its fullest! Put off taking a drink or using for an hour. Do it again for another hour. You'd be surprised how the hours and days will add up!

However, if you just can't stop using then make use of medical facilities that provide detox and rehabilitation. This is one of the most effective methods.

Talk to other addicts about your feelings and your cravings. It is very common to have the urge to use just vanish once you express it to another person. If you keep it hidden in yourself, it is much harder to release it.

Day by day you can stay clean and sober and before you realize it, you will have some solid sobriety under your belt. You will look back in amazement at how you were unable to stop before. You will shudder at the memories of being possessed by your addictive self. You will never want to return to that again.

The medications mentioned above also only help to relieve cravings. They aren't effective unless you undergo therapy, such as group sessions, as well. Abstinence is a must but you cannot stay abstinent unless you undergo a behavioral change.

If your plan is to take one of the drugs just because you think it'll help you drink a bit less, you don't really need this book, at least not yet! If you haven't admitted to yourself that you are an addict and must remain completely abstinent, the medications aren't going to do anything for you in the long run.

Cognitive behavioral therapy is an excellent, proven method that other recovery methods utilize even if they don't use the term. Even 12-step programs have components of CBT embedded in their programs. CBT will become part of your daily program, part of your life. It can change how you perceive not only yourself but the world around you.

Rational Emotive Behavior Therapy (REBT) techniques are similar to CBT in many ways and are actually the basis for cognitive focused therapies. A basic concept of REBT is that rational and dysfunctional ways of thinking, feeling and behaving are contributing to much of human emotional and behavioral defeatism. REBT teaches you how to think and feel rationally. Dialectical Behavioral Therapy (DBT) is an equally powerful set of therapies that has shown substantial promise especially in the treatment of BPD, Borderline Personality Disorder. If you take a step back and regard the average long term addict objectively, most are probably at or near the BPD stage when they first stop using.

CBT/REBT techniques can be found in nearly all therapy models these days. At the very basic level, cognitive/rational emotive behavioral techniques are quite simple. We are what we think. Change your thinking and you change your life. Of course, that is easier said than done and to change your thinking you have to be aware of your thoughts! If you can't change how you think and feel right now, at least stop hurting yourself and accept yourself as you are at this moment.

A change of this magnitude will take time but you have to remain abstinent. Using is only going to hurt you. It helps nothing. You might be able to escape life for a brief time but when you use, you are not yourself. You are letting a substance or behavior control you. You are better than that and reality always is there waiting for you to come back. You simply can not use, no matter what.

Sometimes you will despair of ever being able to think straight because the Beast seems to continually be speaking but in time the Beast will tire. If you don't feed it then it will go to sleep.

If you reach a point of crisis, call someone! Talking with others is a powerful way to release the accumulated energy that is overwhelming you. Taking a deep breath and trying to find a pause between your thoughts is another good way. We'll talk more about that later.

If you relapse, just start over although you aren't really starting over, not from scratch. You've learned things and hopefully you learned something through the relapse. Let's just hope you survive the relapse, many don't. Think about your thoughts and emotions before you used. The important thing is getting up and starting again. Do not despair. Relapse seems to be part of the recovery process for most people. We have to futilely test ourselves over and over sometimes before we are convinced that we are indeed addicts and must remain abstinent.

Staying abstinent is the first step. Learning about your addiction, why you engage in it, changing false beliefs and learned behaviors is next.

# Staying Clean and Sober

*In the depth of winter, I finally learned that within me there lay an invincible summer.*
*- Albert Camus (1913-1960)*


Cognitive Recovery (CR) is a program to help you recognize, accept, take responsibility for, and live freely with your addiction. CR recognizes that no specific higher power is required to recover from addiction but some of us believe in a higher power or are fervent members of a major religion. CR does not demand that you believe in a god and does not demand you be a non-believer.

CR maintains confidentiality. No one will talk about you by name to someone outside of a meeting, at least we certainly would strongly discourage that, but you are free to disclose your addiction and connection with CR if you wish. Some make a point to declare their status as addicts or alcoholics because they feel it is being truly open and honest. This is certainly not for everyone but we certainly appreciate the vital importance of openness and honesty in all we do.

The concept of acceptance is the rock solid base of mindful living, of happiness. Acceptance of your addiction, acceptance that abstinence is the only way to be free of your addiction, acceptance of life as it comes to you.

Rather than teach people to be powerless, we teach people to be responsible for themselves. Can you ever responsibly drink/smoke/use again once you have become addicted? We do not believe that is possible. Perhaps medical science will come up with some marvelous treatment that will free individuals from addiction but right now, abstinence is the only way.

It takes an immense amount of energy being an addict. Calculating when you can use, making sure you have enough money, avoiding overusing at the wrong times, putting up a false front, lying, cheating, stealing, feeling lousy...the list can go on and on. Once we let go of all that behavior we find we have more energy, we have more time, we can truly enjoy life. Being open and honest is like a drink of cool, fresh water after wandering in the desert for years. No more hiding or sidestepping the truth. It is all out there in front for everyone to see. What a marvelous feeling that is.

Living a sober and clean life is a wonderful thing and it is really quite simple. Active addiction is 50% mind and 50% physical. Once you have a substance out of your system, it is 100% mind as long as you don't use again. The addictive mind is part of you and always will be. What you need to do is learn how to recognize it, learn how to resolve conflict and avoid the negative behaviors that most humans seem to wallow in, and learn to accept life on life's terms. It is not a complex thing to do but it can be difficult since we have trained ourselves to fight life for so long. Just be patient and you'll find your days becoming brighter and freer.

An important part of learning to live free is a daily routine. Take time to just not think, to just experience life, to feel gratitude. We humans are such busy creatures with a thousand things to do each day but you must make time to Not Do. Just relax, regard the sky, a tree, listen to music, be aware just of your breathing.

A daily routine will be something very important to your continued sobriety. Starting and ending each day mindfully is important and you can find peace no matter what your situation is. It is all a matter of personal perspective. It will take patience and work but the results can transform your life.

Our lives are so busy at times but most of us can arrange to get up half an hour earlier than we used to just to give us some precious time alone before we have to get involved in the day. That twenty or thirty minutes can make your entire day more focused and positive.

Our lives may not be exactly the way we'd like them to be but at any given moment, absolutely everything can be all right. You might have financial troubles, want a different job, want a higher educational degree, be in an uncomfortable relationship. But, if you pause for a moment and don't think about all that, you can find a moment of peace, of serenity.

Contentment is something difficult for most addicts. Our Beast is never content and we have conditioned ourselves to be the same way with all aspects of our lives. But, if you stop and examine things you can find a lot that you can be content about. Contentment and acceptance doesn't mean that you may not want to change things in your life but that you don't let those things direct your life. You will change things where and when you can but take each moment as it comes.

## The Basic Plan

CR offers a basic plan of how to recover and find your Self again. We show you how we can live as free people, unchained from our addiction.

The first item is often the most difficult initially for newcomers in recovery. They don't want to believe they are different, that they are addicts, that they will never be cured of addiction and that they must always remain abstinent from their drug of choice.

After you manage the first item it is time to examine your life, right any wrongs you may have created in the past, set up some daily routines to follow, be open and honest with others, help others, and live mindfully.

If you follow this program and make it part of your life, your life will become better than you can imagine.

1 - Accept that you are addicted and this is a condition you will always have
2 - Personal Housecleaning/Housekeeping
3 - Working with others
4 - Living mindfully
        — learn to watch your thoughts
        — be aware of thinking and emotions
        — recognize the addictive voice
        — non-judgmental
        — accept life as it is

None of these are difficult to do. The last two are methods of living that every human could (and probably should!) adopt in order to develop a better and happier lifestyle. For addicts, it is critical for us to follow those. Imagine a life where you are free of your addictions. Imagine all the time and money you will have, the peace of mind, the joy of waking up each morning and realizing you are not hungover, that you remember what you did the night before, of not worrying about running out of your drug of choice. Being free of addiction is the most wonderful thing you can imagine. We always end up asking ourselves "Why did it take so long to just let go and stop fighting it"?

Living mindfully is a concept that the entire human race would do well to follow. This basically just means "paying attention". Instead of reacting automatically to things, think and feel first. Experience life without judging it. Know your limitations, know your strengths. Respect others and know that you are part of all of life. Pay attention to your emotions, your thoughts, to others.

We'll touch on each point briefly and go into more detail in subsequent chapters.

## Accept that you are addicted.

It can be difficult to admit that you have a disease or a problem. We want to be normal, whatever that is, and admitting that we have a problem with alcohol or another drug is a tough thing to do for most of us. We want to be in control, in charge, and perfectly fine. Relax, you are ok as you are even if you are addicted to something. This is just how you are and that is alright. If you want to change something in your life, then do it. But, being an addict is not a bad or evil thing, it is just a fact of life.

Being able to admit and accept that this is how you are is vitally important. So many people think they might have a problem but it isn't that bad or they can stop anytime they want, or it isn't affecting their lives THAT much. But, they find that they don't want to do the things they do and yet cannot stop.

If you want to change, you need to face up to the truth. It is up to you.

You can start to change when you accept your disease and know that you will have it for the rest of your life. But, you can get well now! All you have to do is refrain from using. Don't drink, don't drug, don't do whatever it is that you are addicted to.

That can be difficult at first but like anything else, you will find that it becomes easier as time goes by. Many of us reach a point where we feel a deep sense of freedom by making a commitment to never using again. Just doing that alone can empower you and widen your horizons.

# Personal Housekeeping and Housecleaning

Most of us have spent years or decades making a mess of our lives. We find that we react in ways that are not really beneficial to ourselves or others. That is because we've developed self defense mechanisms to simply survive during our using years. We've created a mess of our lives and now it is time to clean it up.

Sit down and list your life assets and liabilities. Make apologies where necessary, amends where needed. Don't beat yourself up but be responsible for your actions. We'll discuss WHY this is important when we reach the Housekeeping chapter.

# Working with Others

It is somewhat ironic that we certainly were able to get ourselves drunk or drugged easily by ourselves but we inevitably need others to get and stay sober and clean. We need others to act as a mirror to our own selves. We have usually lied a lot to others in the past but most of all to ourselves. The addictive self is a part of us and knows us intimately. We require others to see our own selves clearly. As a bonus to this we also can find opportunities to help others which is a very positive thing.

Get a list of people as your own personal support group. Meet with them, go to recovery meetings, telephone them, talk, email, whatever it takes. Do not isolate yourself. We isolated ourselves through our drug of choice. We free ourselves by opening up to the rest of humanity.

Your support group doesn't have to be just addicts! Family, significant other, and close friends can be just as valuable as a fellow addict. The key thing is to have others you can be totally honest with and who will call you out when you start waffling, making excuses, backsliding, or whatever. Those who know you well can point it out if you start that.

There are probably a few people in the world that may be able to recover from their addiction by themselves alone but everyone else needs other people to be successful and happy. Throughout our years of active addiction we shut people out of our lives in an attempt to hide our problems. We trained ourselves to do things alone, to confide in no one, to feel nothing. When we first get clean and sober it is hard to open up again to others but this is an all important step.

If you think you are doing fine by yourself, be wary. That could be your Beast talking. Working with others, talking with others, being honest with others is vital to staying clean and sober.

## Live Mindfully

So much of our lives have been spent in frustration, in fruitless escape, in avoidance, in mindlessness. We reacted to life rather than observing and acting. We let our thoughts rule us, our emotions rule us. We were puppets dancing to the desires of our addiction.

Now is the time to cut the strings, to take charge of our lives. To look at ourselves, at life, to appreciate what is there. We no longer just react but become aware of our thoughts and motivations. We try to not judge life but just accept it. We see the glory and tragedy of being human and accept life as it is.

# Accept That You Are Addicted

**Once we accept our limits, we go beyond them.**
**- Albert Einstein**

This can be a very easy or a very difficult thing for people to do. Sometimes the most obvious problem is transparent to us. With addiction, it can be difficult to admit you have a problem because it is not socially acceptable to be an addict. It also can make you feel different from everyone else. Who really likes to be different?

Without conscious admission of this condition, it will not change. This disease is not just a physical "allergy" to a substance but the abuse has hardwired your brain to react in specific ways. It can be easily qualified as a mental illness. "Whoa, that is even worse!", you say, "Not only am I an addict but I'm crazy?"

Fear not, most humans inhabiting this planet can be diagnosed as having mental quirks that others might call mental illnesses. Your particular mental quirk wants you to abuse a substance and once you start, your physical body creates a powerful craving that is almost impossible to control. As time goes by, you lose even more ability to control since this disease does appear to be progressive.

No, you are not crazy. You have a disease. Just accept that this is how you are and then you can start to heal, to recover. If you have any doubts, re-read the previous chapter **Am I An Addict**. It is not a BAD thing to be an addict. It is just a condition, a disease.

So many of us strive to put the addiction behind us. We want to get better and be able to drink or drug again. We may not even want to do it but we want to be ABLE to. We do not like to be different from others. We do not like the current stigma attached to addicts.

Sometimes it doesn't matter what we want, we just have to accept what IS.

If you think about it, not being able to drink or drug is such a trivial thing. Our society conditions us into believing we have to drink or drug to have a good time but that is not true. Millions of people don't use alcohol or drugs at all and don't miss it. Why should you?

Are you different from others? All that is different is that you can't use a specific substance or engage in a specific behavior. Is that a big deal? No, it is not and if you are a recovering addict and utilize cognitive techniques and mindfulness in your daily life you will find that a lot of "normals" may stomp around angry, frustrated, tired, anxious, envying, and everything else while you don't. You are beyond all that. This is part of your personal power, the acceptance of a lifelong disease.

Acceptance is the cornerstone of sobriety and living freely. Acceptance is the key concept for us all to embrace. So many of us go through life fighting it, trying to mold it into what we want our lives to be and inevitably failing.

Here is an excellent excerpt from the AA Big Book, 4th edition, page 417:
*"And acceptance is the answer to all my problems today. When I am disturbed, it is because I find some person, place, thing or situation -- some fact of my life -- unacceptable to me, and I can find no serenity until I accept that person, place, thing or situation as being exactly the way it is supposed to be at this moment...Until I could accept my alcoholism, I could not stay sober; unless I accept life completely on life's terms, I cannot be happy. I need to concentrate not so much on what needs to be changed in the world as on what needs to be changed in me and in my attitudes."*

Those are powerful thoughts. Through acceptance we gain freedom and we gain happiness. Feeling fear, anger, resentment, joy, envy, sadness, and ecstasy are all human emotions and it is valid to feel them. But, if we obsess on any of them we will end up suffering. We try to just accept every emotion as it is and not dwell on the ones we regard as negative. That also goes for positive emotions. Don't dwell on them or treasure them too greatly because they will pass, as all things do.

If you want to stay sober and clean you must totally and completely accept that you are an addict and must remain abstinent. You cannot lie to yourself and think you might be able to handle a little bit of your drug of choice. You cannot. You must accept this wholeheartedly or you will drink/drug again.

This is often a difficult thing to do and even if you do reach a state of acceptance it can fade over time if you do not renew your personal vow to remain abstinent and accept your addiction. Additionally, if you do not accept life as it comes and fight it, that will only encourage the inner Beast, the addict inside you. The Beast feeds on fear, frustration, resentment, anger, and a host of other emotions. Don't feed it.

Acceptance is all part of living mindfully. If you accept life on life's terms, if you accept what happens and try not to judge it, then life is so very easy. It is when we fight life that it gets "bad". We will go more into acceptance when we talk about living mindfully but acceptance must become the base of your life, the base of your recovery, if you want to stay sober and learn to live free.

Life is a process, an ever changing cycle. Accept the dynamics of life and you can find peace.

# Housecleaning/Housekeeping

*Where is there dignity unless there is honesty?*
*- Cicero (106 BC - 43 BC)*

So many of us go through years or decades of active addiction and we leave our lives somewhat of a wreck. We've lost jobs, had divorces, ignored children, abandoned relationships, been in trouble with the law, committed crimes, and so on. Those past events can fester in our memory. Others have somehow avoided the more dramatic events but inside we are seething with guilt, shame, and fear.

How to let all that go and move on to our bright futures? The best way is to make simple amends to those you have hurt. Often a mere apology to someone is all you need to do. It is an easy thing to do and can release a massive emotional burden.

If we don't "clean house" then we often find we retain resentments, guilt, and fears from our years of active addiction. Those negative emotions stay inside us, jealously harbored by our addictive self. Remember, those are the weapons that the Beast can use with ultimate finesse. To truly free ourselves from the past and stride forward into a bright, sober future we need to release those things.

If we were at fault, as we often were, there usually isn't a lot we can do besides apologize. Oh, we can pay back money we owe, help others we have harmed as well but often it is a matter of living our lives properly that will make the difference, especially to family members. Seeing us staying clean and sober and changing our behavior can be the most rewarding thing we could give them.

We often carry all kinds of rather aberrant self defense mechanisms we created in the past to just survive our using years. We lied at the drop of a hat, we were guilty of stealing, we ignored others and isolated because that seemed safer to us. We shut down our emotions because everything hurt too much to feel. The list can go on and on and is as variable as people are.

Take time over a few weeks or months to really examine the past and list everything you can. Examine yourself now and see what behavioral traits you have carried forward that can be discarded now.

If you don't want to do this housekeeping and you stay sober regardless, that is great. But, most of us need to do this just to sweep away the cobwebs of the past. Once it is done, you can finally let go of fears and guilts that may have been plaguing you subconsciously for a very long time.

Look at your resentments.
Look at your fears.
What makes you angry?
What makes you sad?
What are you ashamed of?
What do you feel guilty about?
What behaviors do you want to change?
What are your strengths and talents?

List all the good things there are about you as well! Too often we focus on the obvious negatives and miss the all important positives. The idea is to write down YOU as you see yourself right now. All the negatives and positives, the past and present. Lay it all out honestly so you can review your own self.

When you have completed your lists, just read through them and think about all the items. Do any of the old things really matter anymore? Do you still feel guilty, ashamed, sad, and fearful about aspects of your past? It is time to release all that. It IS the past and that doesn't exist any more.

When we let go of the past it is as if you have been carrying heavy weights. Each time you let go of something, another weight drops. Each time you apologize sincerely or make an amend, another weight falls away. Before long, you are completely in the present moment, nothing from the past holding you back.

Always remember the past as an instructive tool, a guide. But, let it go and don't let it affect your present life. Most addicts that avoid doing the above will find themselves chained to their pasts and will have problems staying clean and sober. The reason for this is that they are continuing to carry the immense burden of the past guilt, shame, fear, and resentments with them every day.

Why clutter your mind and emotions with old stuff? Just release it and utilize your complete energies in your new clean and sober life!

After you have done this, and you may want to review the process two or three times to make sure you have been thorough, then consider a daily program of housekeeping. Watch yourself throughout the day and see how you behave. Are you kind towards others? Do you listen to others? Do you work honestly and to the best of your ability? Have you allowed things to bother you all day long? It may seem tedious to do this at first but it becomes automatic and you end up not having to carry a lot of emotional baggage with you.

Always remember that the addictive self only sleeps and is always ready to sabotage your sobriety. The addiction does not go away and will always be ready to become active again. This is no real burden though as long as you "keep your house clean".

No one can expect to be 100% after spending years in active addiction. It will take time to do the initial housecleaning. Sometimes you may need to revisit things several times to completely "let go" of it. Some experiences hang on tenaciously and require care and persistence to turn them into mere memories.

But, YOU have the power to do this. There may be a sense of powerlessness when you are actively using but if you remain abstinent you have the power to change your life. This power comes from within and is enhanced and supported by working with others. It could take years to live naturally again after years or decades of actively using, of being caught in the disease. Give yourself time and educate yourself about addiction. Be good to yourself.

Here is a list of character traits and behaviors you can investigate about yourself. Take time to review the list and even take the time to write out each line item with a brief response. Do the same thing six months from today, one year from today. Compare the three sets of answers and you might be surprised.

Feel free to add more items to the list that you might feel pertain specifically to yourself.

# Questions to ask yourself about attitudes and behavior

- If I have tried and failed, can I use what I have learned?
- Am I realistic about my abilities and limitations?
- Am I willing to admit there is room for improvement in my relationships with my family and friends?
- Can I take a stand and express my opinions diplomatically?
- Have I truly accepted addiction as a mental illness?
- Have I learned that no matter what events may occur, no matter what other people may do, I can always choose my attitude?
- Am I wise enough not to expect a partner not to fill all my emotional needs?
- Do I accept responsibility to do something about my problems as they arise?
- Do I set my goals realistically?
- Can I relax when I am by myself?
- Have I kept an open mind, willing to learn no matter what?
- Can I apologize when I'm wrong?
- Do I treat myself well physically, mentally, and spiritually?
- Do I associate with emotionally healthy people?
- Do I enjoy my own company?
- Do I realize that a healthy form of self-love is needed in my relationships with others?
- Am I consistent in my loving attitude toward my friends and family?
- Am I open and honest in my relationships?
- Do I know the difference between detachment and indifference?
- Have I let go of the people and situations I cannot change?
- Do I let others know the real me?
- Have I developed a tolerant, easy-going attitude toward

myself?

- Am I tolerant of others?
- Do I expect others to make special allowances for my behavior?
- Am I able to say no?
- Are my responsibilities to myself kept in good balance with my desire to reach out to others?
- Do I make an effort to consider the needs of others as well as my own?
- Can I compromise realistically?
- Do I avoid judging others?
- Have I eliminated the shoulds and oughts from my vocabulary?
- Do I respect the feelings and experience of others?
- Have I developed some sense of my right to be treated with dignity?
- Do I have patience with myself?
- Can I patiently teach others what I have learned, appreciating their willingness to learn?
- Can I be accommodating and still maintain my self-respect?
- Do I understand that reality is what is happening, not what I think or feel is happening?
- Do I make my own decisions?
- Do I try to understand another's position, even though I may not agree with it?
- Am I comfortable in my social interactions with others?
- Once a conflict is over and I have expressed my anger, can I let go?
- Can I avoid blaming others and accept responsibility for my own actions?
- Do I look for the best in each situation and person that I encounter?

- Do I recover quickly from disappointment?
- Do I listen attentively when others are talking or am I just waiting my turn to speak?
- Do I know the difference between asking for help and imposing?
- Do I treat others kindly, considering their feelings?
- Do I see value in simply lending a listening ear to someone in need?
- Can I accept the love that others offer to me?
- Am I conscientious and tactful in my interactions with others, always considering their feelings?
- Are my feelings expressed in appropriate ways?
- Do I try to say what I mean and mean what I say?
- Do I do what I have promised to do?
- Do I avoid rationalizing or justifying my faults?
- Can I be completely honest, not lying to myself or others?
- Can I admit to others and myself when I am wrong?
- Do I know that a humbling experience is not a humiliating one?
- Can I share another's problems without worrying about them?
- Do I see value in talking to someone about my fears?
- Am I willing to focus on living in the present, in the moment?
- Do I realize that willingness to do something is the first step to actually doing it?
- Do I realize that procrastination often leads to justification for missed opportunities?
- Do I have a purpose in my life?
- Can I discipline myself in a healthy and comfortable way so that I can accomplish things?
- Do I avoid feeling responsible for others lives, but see myself as having responsibilities to others?

- Do I appreciate my talents and abilities?

That is a long but fairly comprehensive list of basic attitudes. Don't just read the question and come up with a quick answer. Spend time determining what is completely true and real. Write down your answers and save them for review at a later date. This is homework to study for the test of how you live your life so be thorough and brutally honest with yourself. It can help to go over all of this with another person you trust. This is quite optional but it is easy for our addictive self to hide things from our conscious self. We can minimize or make excuses or just outright ignore things. But, if we speak openly of our past, we can accept and release it all. This is not a confession, this is learning who we are.

In CR, we don't regard ourselves necessarily as "flawed" but we do admit it when we have done wrong, when we have gone astray from a way of life we would consciously choose. We accept responsibility for our own actions. We can accept our past and move on to our future.

# Working With Others

*When we do the best we can, we never know what miracle is wrought in our life, or in the life of another.*
*- Helen Keller (1880-1968)*

A vital concept in addiction recovery is working with others. Trying to beat your addiction by yourself is incredibly difficult since you are struggling with your inner addict and often you are not aware of how you are behaving, where your mind is going, or what you are feeling. It is so easy to start sliding towards active addiction with hardly realizing it. Others you are close to can notice changes in your behavior and point it out even when you don't recognize it.

Working with others is a very powerful activity. When you are with other addicts there is a shared commonality that you all have gone through. Just knowing you are not alone is a powerful concept to support you. Helping others strengthens the positive in you and makes you stronger. Just attending meetings is immensely helpful. I cannot count the number of times I have heard people talk about how mysterious it is that just coming to a recovery meeting will brighten their outlook and relax them. Troubles and worries will drop away and they leave the meeting with a better perspective.

There is no mystery here, it is just the natural result of being open and honest with others like you. You do not have to carry all your burdens by yourself. There are others there that understand and have gone through the same. Also, feeling part of something is an inherent need of all humans.

There is a theory called "limbic resonance" as well. This theory postulates that we human beings are designed to react, or resonate, emotionally to one another on a neurological level. According to this theory, we are hard wired to react to each other's emotions and behavior. If we consider this phenomenon, then it is clear that it can amplify the positive effect of support groups. Many people focused on a single goal and all supporting one another. Is it any wonder people "mysteriously" feel better after a recovery meeting? The empathy derived from the entire group is a self sustaining beneficial result.

We have deceived ourselves for so long that it is difficult to trust our every thought. Thus, the emphasis on cognitive awareness and living mindfully, watching your thoughts and tracking the origin. But, it is so easy for us to gloss over or minimize something whereas another person might see it plainly.

If there are no secular recovery group meetings in your area, go to 12-step meetings. You can almost always find one of those! You do not have to accept their specific program but you can recognize that the attendees are people like you who are trying to stay clean and sober. There is a lot of honesty and help in any meeting if you are open to it. If you go to meetings and keep yourself closed in and isolated you will receive little. It takes an open mind and heart to receive the positive energy that is there. Of course, meetings vary and you may have to search around to find one you are comfortable with. But, until you can find/start up an CR meeting, a 12-step one can help a lot.

Just talking to another addict on the phone is a major benefit for the same reason as going to meetings. You can be totally honest and not be afraid of someone misunderstanding or not understanding at all. Another addict will just understand and even if they may not totally relate to your particular situation, they have been in similar ones.

By helping others and talking to others, we can greatly facilitate our own recovery. The mere opening up of yourself to others honestly will help you. Too long have we isolated and hidden from the world. If we commit ourselves to being part of the world, we are letting go of part of the addictive disease that used to dominate us.

Note that working with others is not limited to other addicts! Talking with non-addicts, helping them, giving your time to your friends and family, those are all ways to "get out of your own way". Having people you trust that you can say anything to is vital to our mental health. Many people don't go to recovery meetings but you can guarantee that they do talk to other people.

Doing charity work is an excellent way to get "outside yourself". Help coach a Little League team, or volunteer your time for any number of charitable organizations in your area. There is no limit to this type of activity.

The point is to focus on others and not yourself. We addicts need to turn the focus outwards in certain aspects. Focusing on our own selves can be a very good thing but it can be treacherous if our inner Beast pulls us in completely and we isolate, shunning others. If you find yourself isolating, not talking to others, then you need to be very concerned.

Note the first sentence of this chapter. It truly is vital for us to work with others. A very common pattern among addicts before a relapse is to start withdrawing and isolating. By keeping yourself actively engaged with others, you keep the Beast at bay.

# Commitment

*Anyone can dabble, but once you've made that commitment,*
*your blood has that particular thing in it, and it's very hard*
*for people to stop you.*
*- Bill Cosby*

Some recovery groups prefer a daily commitment to not use.
Others may want to expand this to a lifelong commitment. This is
an entirely personal decision for you to make but a commitment
is something that is necessary.

Making a daily commitment reflects a focus on staying clean and
sober just one day at a time. You don't have to think about
tomorrow, next month, or a year from now. All you have to do is
focus on the day.

But, another perspective is a lifetime commitment. Instead of
just focusing on being sober each day, imagine a lifetime of
sobriety that stretches before you. It is like standing on a hilltop
and looking over a grand vista that stretches for as far as you can
see. Imagine the possibilities that lie before you! Many like this
approach much better than the comparison of standing in a
valley, only seeing a few feet ahead of you because of all the
trees. With a daily commitment you only see a few trees but with
a lifetime commitment you can see the whole forest and
appreciate it for all it encompasses.

Making a lifetime commitment can change your perspective
completely if you do it with complete sincerity. You are no longer
an ex-user, you are simply a non-user. It gives you a deeper sense
of freedom and strength when you can look to the future and
know that whatever occurs, you will not have to deal with using a
drug again.

Whether you choose a daily or longer term commitment, be sure
to commit! There are no half measures here. You stay sober or
you don't.

Making a commitment empowers your decision to be clean and
sober and can give you strength and willingness when you need it
most.

# Cognitive Behavioral Therapy

*Little progress can be made by merely attempting to repress what is evil; our great hope lies in developing what is good.*
*- Calvin Coolidge*

Cognitive-Behavioral Therapy is a form of psychotherapy that emphasizes the important role of thinking about how we feel and what we do. CBT is a widespread, effective method of treating disorders, such as alcoholism, depression, post traumatic syndrome, and so on. Elements of CBT can be found in most therapeutic systems.

Cognitive-behavioral therapy does not exist as a unique therapeutic technique. The term cognitive-behavioral therapy is a very general term for a classification of similar therapies. There are several approaches to cognitive-behavioral therapy, including Rational Emotive Behavior Therapy (REBT), Rational Behavior Therapy, Rational Living Therapy, Dialectic Behavior Therapy (DBT), and others.

CBT is based on the cognitive model of emotional response, that our thoughts cause our feelings and behaviors. It isn't the external things such as people, places, situations, or events that cause our feelings but how we personally react and think about those.

CBT is usually considered to be one of the most rapid therapies in regards to achieving results. This is what the addict wants to hear! We usually are impatient types that want everything now! Note that we are not talking instant results but if you focus on CBT practices you can achieve substantive results in a relatively short time.

CBT does not tell you how to feel but gives you a way to examine your feelings and change them. If you are to change yourself, you must know yourself. We learn to confront our problems calmly rather than let the event upset us. If we just react to an event then we have doubled the problem. When we learn to more calmly accept problems, we feel better and put ourselves in a better position to use our intellect, our knowledge, and energy to resolve the problem.

CBT uses an inductive methodology. This is an exercise in perspective. As an example, you might be sure that certain people are angry at you. But, if you remain calm and talk about this to someone else, you might be able to say, "They might not be angry at me. I may just perceive it that way. They might be angry at someone else or just in a bad mood that day." Instead of accepting an immediate feeling or perception as the absolute truth, it is important to examine possibilities.

The inductive method encourages us to regard our thoughts and emotions as being possibilities that can be put to the question and examined. If we have new information concerning a situation, we can change our thoughts, feelings, and behaviors based on the new information.

Examples of this are common sayings like "All lawyers are cheats." or "All politicians are crooks", "No one cares about me", or "Life sucks and then you die". If you really examine those statements, acquire further information and examples, you might just find out that you were wrong. What is wonderful is that you simply change your point of view and you don't have to feel bad or embarrassed about it.

CBT is focused on proven assumptions that most emotional and behavioral reactions are learned ones. Thus, the goal is to unlearn unwanted reactions and to learn new ways to react to life.

How many of us have developed ways of reacting to life that originated from what appeared to be rational self-survival mechanisms that we created when we were actively using? How many addicts found it difficult to be honest, especially when a family member asked, "Have you been drinking/smoking/using?" We are not born dishonest, we taught ourselves to be that way. Most of our behaviors are learned and the negative behaviors were often learned during our using days.

CBT can be rapidly beneficial because it stresses "homework". Take time to write down issues, thoughts, and behaviors. Write down how you feel. Examine what you have written and compare it with the classic cognitive distortions that you'll read about on the next pages. By utilizing a feedback mechanism such as physically writing (or typing in a computer!) and then analyzing and talking with someone else you can change things quickly because you are able to recognize your distorted thinking patterns and are identifying how you act. Once you have rationally identified your behaviors and reactions, you can start to work on changing behaviors you don't want any more.

That is a quick outline of CBT. It works, it doesn't take much time to show systematic results and it empowers you – the addict. You learn about yourself and make the necessary changes to your life. It would be most useful to actually find a therapist who specializes on CBT and do individual and/or group sessions but this is something you can work on by yourself as well.

## Practicing CBT everyday life

How do you think about yourself? When you wake up in the morning do you groan at the thought of another day or do you look forward to what the day might hold in store for you? Do you think negatively about yourself or positively?

During our using years, we addicts build up an enormous negative self-image. Oh, we are quite good at sublimating this negative self-image with a public ego but inside we don't want to look at ourselves. We also developed scores of maladaptive behaviors and coping mechanisms that are not pertinent or healthy in a sober life.

We find ourselves trying to control life around us because we cannot control that addiction inside. We think of ourselves as weak or useless. In the depths of our addictive insanity we may have committed crimes or done acts we are ashamed or guilty of. Even now, newly clean and sober, we are tied to our past mental beliefs.

The past is just that, the past. It doesn't exist anymore. All you have is right now, this minute. Be proud that you make it through each day clean and sober. That is a huge success! Don't minimize your progress. Focus on the positives.

It is important to become aware of what you think and feel and identify distorted thinking. This can be quite difficult at first since we previously just accepted whatever we thought. But, the key here is to recognize how we think and identify the addictive voice as well as the "normal" distorted thinking that every human seems to engage in. For us, it is critical to do this.

At first it may seem clumsy to start questioning our every thought

63

but rapidly we will gain skill in recognizing distorted thinking and after some practice, it is no effort. It becomes an subconscious method of watching ourselves and when our inner Beast spits out something, we can often identify it immediately. Once identified it usually has no power and must fade away again.

After a short time, basic CBT techniques come naturally to you. It is all part of living mindfully, that we talk about more in the next chapter. Being aware, watching your thoughts and emotions, and not distorting reality.

Following is a list of common cognitive distortions. Read through these and you may be surprised to find yourself exclaiming, "Why, I do/have all of those things sometimes!" That is not only ok to realize it but extremely helpful. Once you know how you automatically react, think, and feel you can starting changing.

- **All or Nothing Thinking**
- **Mental Filtering**
- **Disqualifying the Positive**
- **Mind Reading**
- **Fortune Telling**
- **Catastrophizing**
- **Labeling/Mislabeling**
- **Magnifying or Minimizing**
- **Emotional Reasoning**
- **Shoulds**
- **Over Generalizing**
- **Personalization**
- **Compensatory Misconceptions**

Now let's examine these in more detail.

**Cognitive Distortions or Assumptions**

**All or Nothing Thinking:**
You think of things as black-or-white.
e.g. You think of an event as completely good or completely bad. You don't see the "shades of gray" in every event and don't consider alternatives.

**Mental Filtering:**
You dwell on a single detail, and ignore other information.
e.g. You get a flat tire and you kick the car, cursing the day you

bought the "lemon". You ignore the fact that the vehicle has run flawlessly and had no problems until now.

## Disqualifying the Positive:
You reject positive experiences as "they don't count". You maintain a negative view in spite of contradictory evidence.
e.g. You have entered several poetry contests and received awards or honorable mentions. You just say "I'm no good, I have no idea why I won."

## Mind Reading:
You arbitrarily decide that someone is reacting negatively to you, and don't bother to check this out with them.
e.g. You say hello to someone and they just stare the other direction. You decide the person is a snob, that something is wrong with you, that they are so rude.

## Fortune Telling:
You anticipate that things will turn out badly, or very good, and feel convinced that your prediction is going to be a fact regardless of any evidence.
e.g. You are invited to go to a basketball game but you stay home because you think your friends are just humoring you by inviting you and they don't really want you there, and that your team will probably lose.

## Catastrophizing:
You believe the worst-case scenario will generally happen.
e.g. You avoid a vacation to the beach because you think a cyclone is sure to hit. You can't find your car keys and shout "Nothing is going to go right today!"

## Labeling/Mislabeling:
Instead of describing an error, you attach a negative, generalized label to yourself/others.
e.g. Instead of recognizing that you made a little mistake you label yourself a "Loser".

## Magnifying or Minimizing:
You exaggerate the importance of certain things and minimize other things
e.g. You do a good job at work and exclaim how you are the BEST! You are good at your work but are embarrassed at any praise because "It wasn't anything".

## Emotional Reasoning:
You assume that the way you feel reflects the way things are.
e.g. You didn't get enough sleep and are tired. That makes you

grumpy and down. You think that life will always be a tiring, depressing thing.

## Shoulds:
You believe you must live up to certain expectations. You may have extreme expectations of others.
e.g. I must do this, or I am not good enough. (guilt or shame). They must do this, or they are not worth my time. (anger or resentment.)

## Over Generalizing:
You think of a single negative/positive event as a never-ending pattern.
e.g. You apply for a job and someone else is hired. You think of yourself as useless, unwanted, and doomed to ever get a good job.

## Personalization:
You see yourself as responsible for events around you that you had little/no responsibility for.
e.g. Someone ahead of you has a traffic accident and you are sure you had something to do with it because you were behind them.

## Compensatory Misconceptions:
The belief that you need to inflate your achievements to be socially successful.
e.g. Inflating the amount of income you make to feel important.


These examples just touch on the myriad ways we fool ourselves. There are hundreds of ways we fool ourselves through coping mechanisms. How many of you have feelings of grandisosity? How many times do you have daydreams where you emerge triumphant from overwhealming odds? Where you win the lottery?

 Take time right now to pause and think about how your own thinking can distort reality. Write down everything you can think of so you can remember it and catch yourself when you find yourself using distorted thinking in the future.

Remember that everything is not black and white. What may seem "bad" is just that, something that you currently perceive in a negative manner. Regardless of your situation, it is never completely dark. Always look for alternatives and positives.

# Stinking Thinking

*Be miserable. Or motivate yourself. Whatever has to be done, it's always your choice.*
*- Wayne Dyer*

We all have an abundance of "stinking thinking" that goes on in our head. The trick is to recognize it as it happens and not let it influence reality. Our inner Beasts love stinking thinking because it wears us down, makes us feel dishonest, makes us feel unworthy, or angry, or depressed. If we get wrapped up enough in our own selves, we'll eventually find ourselves wanting to use again to escape the "mess".

Many of cognitive distortions we use are a product of not our rational minds, but our addictive self. Recognizing them when they happen and dismissing such things is vital. If we allow ourselves to wallow in misconceptions we are only feeding the Beast and that is another step towards relapse.

First you have to be aware of your thoughts. If a thought is negative or creates negative emotions, then examine it. Is it real or could it be distorted thinking? Carry the list of cognitive distortions we talked about in the last chapter in your wallet so you can pull it out to cross-check yourself at any time.

It is amazing how something very negative can just vanish when you realize it is an exaggeration. But, sometimes you'll go all day long feeling "under the weather" and be overly sensitive to everything around you. On those days, just remind yourself that you may react unfavorably to just about anything. Try to be patient and not overreact. "Let Go and Just Be".

If you don't get enough sleep one night you might be vulnerable to overreacting the entire next day. Just remind yourself you need more sleep and don't allow your emotions to create a distorted reality.

Distorted thinking is a plague that all humans have. The "Seven Deadly Sins" and all other "sins" are a result of that type of thinking. It is a result of non-acceptance and lack of contentment. It is not feeling ok just being who you are.

Non-addicts might be able to wallow in that sort of thing but addicts cannot afford it. When we indulge in anger, frustration, resentment, self-pity, envy, and all those other negative emotions, we are walking a razor thin line that we can so easily step off of and end up using again. Distorted thinking can lead us to death and destruction so very easily. We must learn to use CBT and other techniques, must live mindfully, or our futures are either dark or non-existent.

We all get negative at times. We will be anxious, depressed, angry, frustrated, envious, or just feel a general malaise. A lot of times we do not know why we feel that way! In order to dissect the emotion and hopefully resolve it you can do the following:

1) Ask yourself: What was I doing? What was the situation? What was I thinking? What was the trigger that caused this feeling?

Often it helps to write down whatever is going through your mind. A free form mind dump, as it were. If you are feeling sad, start listing all the things that might make you feel sad. Don't think hard about this, just start listing things. If you are feeling angry, list the things that are bothering you. You often can find the trigger to your feeling in one of the words/situations you have listed.

2) Ask yourself how unhelpful/non-useful your feeling is. If you are really down in the dumps then you might rate it a 9 out of 10. If you are a bit depressed, you might rate it a 3. A lot of times we seem to automatically classify everything as a 10. Take time to examine the feeling, examine the trigger, and then rate it. That helps put things in perspective and often it helps to clarify the specific, most pressing problem you have.

3) Am I / Was I using distorted thinking? Was I using oughts and shoulds? Was I catastrophizing? Look at the distorted thinking list and see if you were applying any of those. Even if you think you were reacting fairly realistically, it still is ok to experience negative emotions. Just don't dwell on them and let them color your whole outlook.

4) No one is saying that how you are feeling is not valid. But, is it as bad as you currently think/feel? Is there another way to view it? What other ways can you think about it? What constructive thoughts can you come up with concerning this? How can you change your perception of this?

Just by going through the process of identification and analysis of your thoughts and feelings you can often find yourself released of the negative feeling. You realize it wasn't so bad after all. It usually is a great relief to just know WHY you were feeling that way.

Suppose you are feeling really depressed one morning. You apply the steps above and realize that you are feeling down because:

a) you are still in legal trouble because of a DUI you had in the past and that bothers you.
b) your finances are in sad shape and you wonder how you will work yourself out of the hole
c) you are lonely and have no one to share this with

Those are pretty big concerns but you can handle them all, one by one. The legal problems will work out over time. The finances will improve over time. You don't HAVE to be lonely and someday, possibly soon, you will not be. Besides, if you are doing this program correctly, you have a network of people to talk to and don't have to be totally alone.

When you realize all this, the day seems to brighten. You know that you had very good reasons for being down and all together they seemed pretty massive but they will work themselves out. You decide to take a walk and call a friend later.

That is just one of innumerable examples that could be listed here. Aways give yourself room for doubt. Listen to other people and accept that they have a viewpoint. Who in this world is always right after all? Give yourself time to review your thoughts and emotions.

Be wary when you hear yourself express things in absolutes such as "I will NEVER be able to ..." or "This is ALWAYS going to be like this..." and so on. Those are words that can lead you to despair and most likely your inner Beast is expressing them. You know, logically, that there are few absolutes. If there is nothing you can do at the moment but accept a situation, then accept it and think positively of the change you can make happen in the future.

All that sounds easy when you write it out or read it but in actual practice, it can be much more difficult. You may have to let go of a situation over and over. You may have to repeatedly focus on the moment just to keep yourself from being overcome with fear or anxiety. It isn't always easy to do.

Sometimes you just have to accept that something seems unacceptable to you. Life IS and you don't have to like it. That is a somewhat fatalistic perspective but sometimes all you can do is say, "Ok, this is how it is. I don't like it but I can't do anything about it right now."

Sometimes you just have to accept life as it comes. In fact, that is the ideal way to live! If you go through the steps above and still feel badly about something, you can still just accept it. One thing you can be sure of is that your life will change, your feelings will change. They may not change to your personal, preferred schedule but they will change. Nothing stays static.

Our inner addict will make use of everything it can to tear us down, to wear us down, to infuriate us, to depress us, or make us anxious and fearful. Learning to recognize stinking thinking and the addictive voice is how we stay clean and sober.

# Dialectic Behavioral Therapy

*Within each of us lies the power of our consent*
*        to health and to sickness,*
*        to riches and to poverty,*
*        to freedom and to slavery.*
*        It is we who control these, and not another.*
*- Richard Bach*

In the 1970s, Marsha M. Linehan developed therapeutic approaches to treating BPD, borderline personality disorders Dr. Linehan's theory is that the core problem in BPD is emotional dysregulation that has been created from either genetic and/or other biological factors. An emotionally unstable childhood environment is usually a precursor to the condition. DBT is about helping the client learn skills so they can cope with the emotional dysregulation.

You may encounter DBT techniques in therapy sessions, especially if you are in the first three stages of the transtheoretical model of change as we discussed earlier in the book. Many addicts demonstrate obvious aberrant behaviors when they first stop using. We spent so much of our lives lying, cheating, stealing, and living in fear. No wonder we skirt the borders of society. We don't want others to know us and by isolating, we only distorted our realities more.

We won't discuss specific DBT techniques since those are best encountered in a therapeutic environment but DBT has one underlying theme that is critical and supportive to the CR program. Sometimes you have just have to accept life as it is. You may not be able to change it or yourself at this moment but neither do you have to become overwhelmed by people, places, or things.

Some of the time all we can do is just accept that something is "wrong". We don't or can't change our feelings at the moment and we dare not let it sweep us away. So, we just accept it. If we do not continue to harm ourselves through substance abuse then we are ahead of the game.

Accept, validate your feelings and thoughts, be patient and work on change when you can. The first step is to stop self defeating, self harming behaviors. Remain abstinent and be good to yourself.

# Rational Emotive Behavioral Therapy (REBT)

**Happiness is like a butterfly which, when pursued, is always beyond our grasp, but, if you will sit down quietly, may alight upon you.**
**- Nathaniel Hawthorne**

Rational emotive behavior therapy (REBT) is an empirically based psychotherapy which focuses on the resolution of emotional and behavioral problems.

The intent is to enable people to lead happier and more fulfilling lives. REBT was created by the psychotherapist and psychologist Albert Ellis. REBT was the first form of cognitive behavior therapy and was founded in the mid-1950s.

A fundamental premise of REBT is that people get emotionally upset by their perceptions of reality. These perceptions come about through their language, beliefs, societal conditioning and personal philosophies about the world. In REBT the A-B-C-model of psychological disturbance and change is taught.

**A.** Something happens.
**B.** You have a belief about the situation.
**C.** You have an emotional reaction to the belief.

To work through irrational beliefs REBT uses Dispute, Insight, and Acceptance techniques.

With the **Dispute** technique the therapist or individual questions the beliefs to determine irrational or distorted thinking.

With **Insight** the individual can realize that they mainly get upset because of their inflexibility. By not allowing room for change or doubt, we aren't open enough to accept other viewpoints. We also hold onto the inflexible beliefs even if new information may suggest that we are wrong. Another facet of the Insight technique is that it takes work to change things. Issues don't magically go away, you have to make some effort.

**Acceptance** has several points to reflect upon:

- I am a fallible human being; I have my good points and my bad points. There is no reason why I must be perfect.

- Despite my good points and my bad points, I am basically

no different than any other human being. Other people may treat me unfairly from time to time. It just happens.

- The people who treat me unfairly are no different than any other human being. They are just people.

- Life doesn't always work out the way that I'd like it to.

- Life may not always go the way I want it to but I can always bear what occurs. Life might not be fair but who ever said it would be?

Those points provide a deep insight to our own distorted way of thinking. Those points would be excellent to include with the earlier CBT self checks we discussed.

This book does not intend to give a step by step process of how to recover using REBT. The S.M.A.R.T. Program is exactly that and can be found at http://www.rebtnetwork.org/, and http://www.smartrecovery.org/. The REBTNetwork site has ebooks that are very useful to download and read and the smartrecovery.org site is full of valuable material. I've given this brief introduction to emphasize the importance of it.

# Living Mindfully

*Past and Future are a duality of which Present is the reality.*
*The now-moment alone is eternal and real.*
*- Wei Wu Wei*

Mindfulness can be thought of as a kind of nonjudgmental, present-centered awareness. Every thought, feeling, or sensation that arises in the field of attention is acknowledged and accepted as it is. The key here is acceptance without judgment, a detached awareness. It is like walking through life with your eyes open whereas previously you had been stumbling through life with your eyes closed, bouncing from one life event to another.

You realize that in the past you were not seeing the world, not seeing others, not seeing yourself. You were just floating along half awake. That may be acceptable for some people but addicts especially have to learn to be aware.

When you are living mindfully, you do not allow the past to bother you, you do not let the unknown future concern you. You live in the moment and you do not judge the moment. This sounds rather impossible and unrealistic to most people. But, for an addict this could be a blessed state. Your past does not haunt you, you do not have to worry about the future, all you need to do is focus on the NOW. The present moment is all that truly exists. Everything else is past or future and is meaningless to the present moment.

Pause right now and be aware of your self. You are probably sitting down, holding this book in your hands. You may have financial problems, relationship difficulties, legal problems, anxieties, fears, or any number of other situations in your life but do they really exist at this current moment? No, not really. They are events not in this particular moment and they do not actually exist.

That might sound a bit mystical but in the split nanosecond you are reading THIS word, they materially are non-existent. They only exist after you think back about them or think into the future about them.

An excellent book to read that explains this concept perfectly is

"The Power of Now" by Eckhart Tolle. He describes this mindset in an effortless, easy to understand manner. Many others have talked about this but when I read Tolle's description of this technique, it just all made sense.

Live in the present moment, and you can let go of the past and not worry about the future. As you sit here become aware of your body, your emotions, your thoughts, your surroundings. Each second that passes changes your personal existence, your personal now. Is there anything truly wrong with the present moment? Of course not, it is all that exists and it doesn't matter if you are suffering from cancer, or have just lost a loved one, or are scheduled to be imprisoned, or have a horrible craving to use some substance...that does not exist in the present moment.

Can you see how this is such a powerful way to live? If you are a smoker trying to quit, you don't want to light up another cigarette. That next cigarette is in the future and it does not exist. You do not have to do it because you can move from each moment to the next and be free of the craving to smoke. This is not an easy thing to do because we are not accustomed to living in the moment. We are accustomed to trying to live in the past, the present, and the future all at once. No wonder we rarely find peace.

Most of us cannot exist easily in this sort of mindset and it takes a lot of practice to allow ourselves to experience even a bit. There are ways to learn how to live mindfully.

Whatever you are doing, do it and nothing else. If you are mowing the yard, reading a book, washing the dishes, working your job, do just that and do not think of the past or the future. Do not think of what might be or what was. Do what you need to do now and only that.

Be aware of your thoughts and emotions. It is common to have ones mind run on constantly as you do something but you can focus on the pause between thoughts and lengthen that interval until you are just Doing, just BEing.

One extremely simple and valuable technique is to just be aware of your thoughts. This is also a critical part of the CR program. If you cannot become aware of your thoughts and emotions, you will probably use your drug of choice again for you will continue to make the same mistakes. If you do learn to watch your thoughts and recognize them, to analyze them, you can then be the master of them.

Watch the thoughts coming into your mind. As you gain experience in being aware of each thought try focusing on the tiny gap before the next thought comes. Seize that moment of non-thought and focus completely on it. When you do this, you achieve a connection with your deeper self, the self that is beyond thought, beyond mind. It is amazing how tranquil, how right it feels to just not think sometimes. It is easy to do and becomes easier the more you practice it. This is one of the techniques that Eckhart Tolle describes as well in "The Power of Now".

Most people think incessantly and are usually unaware of it. This is how we have always lived and even when we think we are experiencing "quiet times" our minds are still busy analyzing, recording, and digesting.

Try to just seize that moment between thoughts and let the quietness wash over you. Feel your body relax and feel the connection you have with the world. The key is disconnecting your mind for a moment and just existing as you are for one instant of time.

All you need to do is to accept the fact that your life just exists from moment to moment. The past is gone and while you may have memories, they are just that, thought forms that have no real substance. The future is nothing to worry about because it may never happen, at least in the way you might imagine.

If you practice mindfulness you can find peace. Focus on what you are doing at any moment in time. As you walk across the yard be aware of the stems of grass moving gently in the breeze. Be aware of the sounds around you. Be aware of the sky and clouds. Be aware. Be mindful.

To evolve into the kind of human being you want to be, to regain the innocence, the wonder, the acceptance of life, you need to be mindful. You also need to practice being mindful because it doesn't come easily to most of us who are immersed in our busy schedules.

Daily meditation is one of the most important things you can do. There are many ways to meditate. You can sit and be aware of your breathing, you can reach for that space between thoughts, you can just observe nature in all its aspects, you can listen to music (just don't analyze it!), the list is pretty much endless.

You must also understand that you have to have patience. We addicts are not known for being patient. We are instant gratification types of people. But, as you practice mindfulness and meditation, as you practice watching your thoughts and resolving emotions, you learn to be patient without apparent effort.

You are going to experience a personality change, an enlightenment of sorts. But, it takes time. You will sigh and wonder if meditation is helping. You'll be tempted to put it off and at times you'll just say, "This isn't doing anything.'" But, this is a cumulative effect that builds the more you meditate, the more that you practice mindful living. If you are alert to your thoughts and feelings you'll note that you are more peaceful, you think better, you are quieter inside and happier regardless of your situation in life. You'll begin to accept life as it comes and that will feel right and natural. Just give it time and you will allow the universe to unfold within you.

Another aspect of living mindfully is being responsible. This will come naturally as time goes on but it doesn't hurt at all to pay special attention to it. Be responsible for your own self, your actions and words. Be responsible for your own thoughts and feelings.

As your grasp on mindfulness grows you will find your natural instincts of honesty, compassion, humility, and appreciation will flower. Take time to encourage these qualities in yourself. Every single day is a day full of things to appreciate.

Mindfulness is something to be experienced. Words used to describe it always fall short of the actual experience but they are all that we can use to share the concept with others. It takes practice to actually live it.

Mindfulness is non-judgmental observation of life. When you are observing your existence mindfully you are not criticizing or judging. You are balanced and centered. This is an ideal state but most people have a difficult time being non-judgmental. We want to classify things as good or bad. While such classifications can be useful to us, they also lead us to form opinions based on limited experiences and often are flawed.

We all perceive the world through our own personal perceptual filters that are created from our life experiences. Such filters are affected by childhood upbringing, by societal mores, by religion, and personal experience. Our perceptual filters are also changing constantly as we experience new things. But, what we perceive is not always what IS.

If we try to live non-judgmentally we observe without our perceptual filters. This is a nearly impossible task initially because we are conditioned to use our past to judge the present and future. But, if we can be objective rather than just interpreting everything subjectively through our perceptual filters then we can see what really is.

Mindfulness is a non-conceptual awareness. When you are living mindfully, you are not involved with concepts.

Mindfulness is Now. It takes place in the present moment. You do not expect, do not try to attain, you just experience.

Mindfulness is awareness of experiences and changes and is a participatory observation. The individual is both a participant in life and an observer as well. If you watch your emotions or physical sensations, then you are also feeling them at the same time. If you are living mindfully then your mind will not get stuck in obsessive patterns. You notice your emotions and see how thoughts feed emotions that feed events that, in turn, feed thoughts again. Because you can notice these things, you can break the automatic cycle and free yourself. This is so important for an addict since relapse happens because we do not notice the addict part of us gaining power. By living mindfully, you become aware and break the cycle before it grows too strong.

No one can truly live in pure mindfulness every moment of the day. Most people have trouble experiencing mindfulness at all and only through practice, through meditation, through grasping the spaces between thoughts can you give yourself enough breathing room to do so.

That is what meditation is for, to give you a chance of experiencing mindfulness. Mindfulness can simply be paying attention. Slow the brain down, interrupt the constant analysis, and just experience life.

This does not mean you walk through life with a bemused, vacant expression on your face. You experience life to the fullest, all the joy, fear, sadness, and everything else that there is. But, you don't get enmeshed in judging or weighing what happens. You pay attention to what is not only happening around you, but what is happening in you.

When you find yourself doing this automatically you will find yourself happier, calmer, more capable, and open to the joy that life has to offer.

# Living Sober

**You are never given a wish without also being given the power to make it true. You may have to work for it, however.**
**- Richard Bach**

You've admitted that you are addicted and made a commitment to stay clean and sober. You have examined your past and present behaviors and made amends if those were necessary. You may have areas in your life that you want to change. You are trying to live a clean and sober life.

Come up with a daily schedule that includes quiet time for you to just not think. Also find time to practice CBT type checks. Look at your thoughts and feelings and determine if they are products of your mind or your addictive self. These types of self-checks become automatic and you will hardly be aware of it.

Wake up each morning and rejoice that you do not have to use today. Remember the mornings you woke up swearing you would not drink/drug today but found yourself doing it later anyway? You do not have that assaulting you this day and that is something very wonderful.

Regard each day as an opportunity to learn. Be sure you make time to relax and recreate and you won't feel guilty about doing it because you are more productive than you have been in the past. You may find yourself re-interested in old hobbies that you let go of in the past because of your addiction demanding the majority of your time. You may become interested in new hobbies.

You need to feel proud of yourself. There are millions of people who are still active addicts. You are making a difference not just for yourself but for family and friends.

It isn't going to be easy to shed deeply conditioned behaviors though. You will find yourself slipping back into old ways of thinking at times. It could take years to free yourself of some deeply ingrained habits but every day that you focus on your sober life will be better.

Don't despair about not being perfect right away. In fact, you'll never be "perfect" but perhaps it is a useful ideal to work toward. Be as good as you can be and that is good enough for today. Give yourself room and time to change. It isn't going to happen overnight so be satisfied with small changes, bits of progress.

Something important to remember is that **It's not all about you.** To live in a sober manner means reaching out to others and in the process we find that we end up caring more than we knew we did. The Beast always wanted you to think the world revolved around you in one way or another but we all are just participants together in life.

If someone cuts you off in traffic don't get angry, be concerned that the driver is probably headed for an accident if they aren't more careful. If you have to wait for a doctor's appointment don't get impatient. Instead, consider how busy the doctor must be! Getting out of our own heads, regarding our own selves and our own lives as less important in the great scheme of things is sober living.

Often we run mental videos on situations that are past, current, or in the future. We rehearse our lives forwards and backwards when we should just be living each moment. When you find yourself discussing, arguing, re-living something in your mind just take a deep breath and catch that moment between thoughts. Just don't think about it and try to break the mental-emotional cycle. Running our brains at full speed all the time is definitely not what we want or need.

Face each day's events square on and avoid judging what is going on. Too often we will wrap ourselves up in judgments and fantasy and miss out on life altogether.

## Lists

Sometimes we have an undefined worry or nagging feeling that makes us uncomfortable. We may feel edgy or nervous. We can't put our finger on the problem. One of the best things you can do in this situation is sit down and start listing what might be bothering you. List anything and everything you can think of. If you do this without judging, just letting the thoughts come out of you it is likely you'll suddenly say "Aha! That is bothering me" as an item appears. Keep going though until you feel you have finished listing the possibilities.

Next, list all the good things in your life, the things you appreciate. Don't neglect this step! It will often put the possible negatives you listed into perspective.

When you are finished with the list just think about it and a lot of times you will realize that undefined worry has gone. Whatever it was, it doesn't really matter all that much at this moment.

The rationale is that by taking time to stop thinking only in our heads and making ourselves put words down on paper we can break the mental cycle and actually see what is going on inside ourselves.

## Be Wary

The following goes for anyone, no matter how much sobriety they have, but it especially important for those just learning to live a sober and mindful life. Be wary of past lifestyles, be wary of triggers. We all have specific triggers whether they are external or internal situations that can threaten our sobriety.

If you were a drinker, stay out of bars. Don't hang around friends who are drinking or drugging. Make sure your own home space is clean of anything you might abuse, even things like mouthwash with alcohol in it, or cooking sherry. Don't underestimate the power and insanity of your Beast. It will be happy to use anything to get started again.

Avoid events where alcohol is served, at least during the first several months to a year or so. During the first year you have a lot of re-thinking and re-programming to do. You are not completely safe in your responses to situations. If you must attend such a function, such as a party or dinner, let people know you do not drink and ask for coffee, tea, or a soft drink. If possible, serve yourself so there aren't any mistakes! Believe me, there are lots of people who don't drink just as a personal preference, this is nothing to be nervous about. If you do get antsy in such a situation, leave as early as you can. You don't have to try to be a hero and white knuckle it if you start feeling uncomfortable. You are ALREADY a hero by not drinking or drugging.

A lot of us used alcohol or other drugs when we got ill. It was a handy excuse. Be wary if you get a cold or flu or if you get injured. The Beast loves pain and distress because when we are not feeling our best, it could have more control.

Avoid food cooked in wine, or flaming desserts. Most of the time we told ourselves we just enjoyed the flamboyance or taste but we mainly were just trying to get a bit more of something into our systems. Watch out for pure extracts such as vanilla. Those can be up to 40% alcohol and many an alcoholic has started adding a bit of vanilla to their coffee "just for the flavor" and soon discovered they were running to the store much too frequently to buy more vanilla.

If you have been prescribed medication by a doctor, take only the exact dosage required at the stated times. If you have to take pain pills after a surgery, you might let someone else give them to you at the appropriate times. If you are on tranquilizers or a mood leveler, take no more than you are supposed to. It is too easy for addicts to rationalize and take an extra pill or two.

When holidays, birthdays, anniversaries, or other like events arrive, be wary! Those days were the ones we most often used as an excuse to meddle with our drug of choice. How many people used the Superbowl weekend as a grand excuse to get completely wasted? How many used Christmas, or their own birthday? Those days can be triggers for many of us.

Be wary even if wonderful things happen to you. That might sound strange but the Beast can use happy emotions just as easily as negative ones if you let it. You might get a raise at work and you hear that silent whisper in your mind, "I should celebrate!" Sure, celebrations are good things but you can do that without poisoning yourself.

Everyone has their own triggers. It would serve you well to realize this and take time to sit down and write out all the possible ones you can think of. Talk to others and keep your list of triggers in mind.

Be wary of your feelings and your reactions to things that happen in life. This is all part of living mindfully. You must be aware, because if you are not, resentments or other negative emotions will creep quietly into your subconscious and just grow as time goes by. The trick is to be aware of your thoughts and emotions, resolve what you can, and accept everything.

## Emotions

When you first get sober and clean, you will find you have a lot of work to do. You will go through many changes and challenges. Your emotions will often run rampant at times and go through extremes. You might be joyous and triumphant one day and feel as if you simply can't go on the next morning. Your emotions will level out as time goes by. For most addicts, the emotional roller coaster starts within the first few months of sobriety and can last several months more. This is a natural phenomenon that occurs to everyone.

Remember that emotions are mutable, changeable. What you feel at any one moment will change because nothing continues forever. Change is inevitable and this is actually a powerful concept to hold onto. If you are feeling sad, anxious, afraid, or depressed then don't worry about it because those feelings will change for the better. The inverse is true as well. If you are happy and content, that will change too so treasure the moments when you have positive emotions and remind yourself of them when you feel a downward trend.

Because our emotions are often unruly the first several months into recovery, it is usually advised to make no sudden changes. Change is a marvelous thing but an emotional surge may cause us to make changes when we probably should just stay as we are for awhile.

Think before you act. You might be tired of your job, it is boring and is going nowhere. You can do better than that. But, if you just quit or jump into some other job you might find yourself worse off. Think about making changes before you do them. Talk things over with others. See if your feelings change and rationally examine your options.

The same goes for relationships. Our active addictive days saw us abusing our relations with other people. We were thoughtless, selfish, angry, and fearful. Now that we are sober we might feel we are fine now and deserve a good relationship. We certainly do deserve that but at what cost? Do we sever a longtime relationship with someone who stuck with us through the bad times because we found someone else that we like better now? If we have been single, do we jump into a relationship that we think is perfect?

As in anything else, stop and think. Talk it over with others. Relationships are probably the toughest things to do right in this life. Dealing with another human being on an intimate and honest basis takes someone who is honest with their own self. Give yourself time. If it is a good thing, it will be better when you are really ready.

You may look back at your past and be filled with disgust at what you did. How could you have treated yourself and others that way? You may find your financial situation teetering or in ruins. You look at yourself and feel despair. One perspective to always keep in mind is that you are not drinking/drugging now. Your life is 200% better than it was when you were. You can ALWAYS make changes in your life and the past really doesn't matter anymore. Your future does.

Remember, what you are feeling at any one moment will change. You may completely believe that a situation is as you feel it but a few hours later that may change. Always give yourself time before reacting. Work on patience and deliberation. Always be gentle with yourself.

## Diet and Exercise

When we first start on the road to recovery, we often find that we have neglected our health. In our using days we focused more on our substance of choice than anything. It is any wonder that we may be overweight, underweight, out of shape?

Health is important to anyone but especially to newly recovering addicts. At least take a multivitamin every day and it certainly won't hurt to initially take extra C, E, and a B complex. Visiting your physician for a checkup is always a good idea and you can discuss vitamin therapies with the doctor after they find out what kind of condition you've put your body into.

Stay away from sugary foods and other empty calories. Focus on green leafy vegetables, fruits, and whole grains. Protein is necessary and can be acquired through meats and dairy products as well as other sources. Some of the best and complete protein you can get is through eating eggs, or beans and rice.

Try to eat several small meals a day rather than two or three large ones and make your evening meal one of your smaller ones. Your stomach and digestive system have been abused for quite some time and you need to take care of them now.

There are a lot of books and information on the internet about proper diet so we won't try to prescribe a perfect diet for you. Your body is unique and will require specific nutrition. Speaking to your doctor about diet would be advantageous.

Exercise is another thing that is vital. How many of us only exercised the arm that lifted a beer can or walked from the living room to the kitchen to pour another drink. How many of us exercised our hands by twisting the top of medicine bottles? When was the last time you took a walk, lifted weights, really stretched?

Exercise is a must if you want to be healthy. You don't need to become a health fanatic or buy a membership with a health club. You also don't want to overdo anything. But, start walking! Start stretching carefully every day. As time goes on you'll find yourself wanting to walk more, perhaps lift weights, do active sports such as basketball, tennis, or something.

We spent a lot of our time sitting and being high. Our newly recovering bodies are, in most instances, really out of shape. Start gentle exercises and increase your efforts as weeks pass.

## Relapse

If you let things slide and physically relapse then don't beat yourself up too much. Addiction seems to be characterized by relapse. Not everyone does relapse but most do at least once. It is as if it takes a few tries at sober living before we can really grasp it and not let go. Living sober means living responsibly, living honestly, and living with the awareness of your thoughts, feelings, and behaviors.

Relapse actually starts a long time before you physically do it. The Beast has been quietly and subtly working on you and afterwards you can usually look back and see what had been going on. You may have even been aware of it happening but felt helpless to stop it. You are NOT helpless though. It usually takes being involved with others to stay clean and sober. Did you slack off on going to meetings of some kind or talking to others? Did you stop reading inspirational literature or skip self-checks? Did you find yourself too busy to give yourself quiet time?

How do you know if you are headed for a relapse? If you start feeling negative about things in your life, or feel depression or anger frequently, if you develop an apathetic viewpoint towards things or feel hopeless at times. Those are definite signs that something is going on that you need to discover and resolve. If you find yourself not talking to other people and avoiding others because you think you don't have the time or just don't want to bother with them; that can be a big sign as well. Finding yourself having thoughts or daydreams of using is also very significant.

Remembering "the good old days" when you could drink or drug is a big sign. Your addictive self, your Beast, is a liar. When you think thoughts of the how nice it would be to just escape for an evening and blur things a bit then you know that your Beast is lying to you again. You know it won't be a simple blur but a headlong plunge into deep impairment.

 Finding yourself obsessing over things is another sign. You might find yourself constantly thinking/doing/talking about politics, sex, food, or anything else. Obsession is often the best method for the Beast to get you into a state of non-acceptance. Once you get into that vicious cycle of non-acceptance you are much more vulnerable.

If you start thinking about drinking or drugging, call someone! You might be one hundred percent sure you would never pick up again but the fact you are having thoughts about using means the Beast is exerting itself again. If you catch yourself having thoughts about how unfair it is that you can't drink or drug anymore, or seemingly random thoughts come into your mind about it, shift your thoughts. Don't dwell on it. If you allow yourself to become fascinated with such thoughts you will only give your inner addictive self more energy to use.

The road to relapse is different for everyone but the above signs are pretty common.

If you do relapse, you don't have to stay actively using. You are not powerless! Just stop using and continue forward. It can seem extremely hard to stop but you can do it. If nothing else, check yourself in somewhere to get detoxed. Call people and explain what is going on. Ask for help. You have the power to stop.

However, all this talk of "power" may encourage the sick addict to believe they can get high one day and "just stop" the next. No, it doesn't work that way. If you consciously, deliberately, start drinking or drugging, you may be in for a long haul. When that happens you have basically given yourself over to your inner demon, your Beast, and it is in charge now. Yes, you do have the power to stop but don't take that as an excuse to use. You might be able to reach out for help or the Beast may be in such control that you will isolate or make excuses. That is why we stress abstinence.

There is a difference between a slip and a relapse. A slip is characterized by an impulse whereas a relapse is characterized by isolation and invalid rationalization. Both are the result of not living mindfully, not being honest with your self. They both have the same result...you use.

If you slip or relapse you don't have to keep using. This bears repeating. You might be at a party and someone hands you a glass of wine or champagne. You pause, shocked for an instant, and then impulsively take a drink. You are helping friends clean out a garage in the summertime and one friend hands you a beer. Sweat streaming down your face, you tilt it back and take a big swallow. Then you realize what you've done.

In all of those cases, don't just shrug and think, "Oh well, I've done it now I may as well keep going." No, at the moment you have really realized what you've done, just stop. Your Beast will be clamoring for More MORE MORE but you can just walk away. Talk to someone about it. I can't stress enough that involving others at this point can be critical. If you try to do it yourself, there is an excellent chance you won't make it.

If you are secretive about a relapse then the chances are very good that you will use again! If not tomorrow, then the next day or the next. Talk to someone as soon as possible. Don't allow the Beast to be secretive. Don't allow it to make you feel complacent or rationalize away the incident.

Most people relapse because they are not talking with others. We begin to isolate or rationalize. We sweep things "under the carpet" instead of facing them. There are a thousand ways for the Beast to insert little time bombs into your mind if you allow it. However, if you are open and honest with other people, the Beast doesn't have a chance to hide things.

It is often said that relapse is part of being an addict. But it doesn't have to be. Relapse happens because your thinking goes awry. You let Beastly thoughts come in. You don't live mindfully, you stress yourself out, you ignore warning signs, you don't observe your thoughts and emotions, you don't talk to others.

Don't beat yourself up if you do relapse. It DOES happen to most of us.

If you've gone on a long bender and consumed lots of your drug of choice you may need to be hospitalized. That is the safest way to detox your body from the poison. There are many of us who would not want that sort of public scrutiny and try to do it ourselves but in severe cases you can die from any number of events during detox such as a stroke or a heart attack. So, be smart and get medical assistance if at all possible.

Just get back into your program. Perhaps you can identify where things started sliding and be forewarned the next time. This disease is so cunning and subtle is often takes quite a bit of time and practice to just identify the addictive voice and how easily it can slip into our lives again.

The big problem with relapse is that it can kill you. You might get drunked up or drugged up and drive your vehicle and kill someone, or yourself. You might use a dirty needle or take too many pills. You might find yourself in jail and facing serious legal consequences. You might injure yourself and bleed out while you lie in a helpless coma. A bit of fear about results can be a good thing.

Meditate, live mindfully, be patient with yourself and the world. Enjoy life and take time to really LOOK at a tree or flower or a lawn full of green grass. Watch the clouds in the sky and enjoy the rain, the sound of wind. You are a part of life and an important part. Make the most of your sober life.

# Spirituality and Religion

*Spirituality exists wherever we struggle with the issue of how our lives fit into the greater cosmic scheme of things. This is true even when our questions never give way to specific answers or give rise to specific practices such as prayer or meditation. We encounter spiritual issues every time we wonder where the universe comes from, why we are here, or what happens when we die. We also become spiritual when we become moved by values such as beauty, love, or creativity that seem to reveal a meaning or power beyond our visible world. An idea or practice is spiritual when it reveals our personal desire to establish a felt-relationship with the deepest meanings or powers governing life.*
*- Robert C. Fuller*

CR, like other secular recovery groups, does not require a god to get and keep sober. You can definitely be good without god and you can definitely get and stay sober without one. If you have a particular religious faith then by all means use your beliefs if they help. Religion can be a powerful force in people's lives. Humans have always searched for "the divine" in one way or another.

We recognize that there is very little personal control in the universe but the addict, lacking nearly all control over substances, strives to find self-mastery in all other parts of their life. That creates a wealth of negativity and only creates more problems. You cannot fight addiction, you have to accept it.

How do you "let go" and just accept, or surrender? Who do you let go to or surrender your life to? A god? If you want to, that is fine. If you don't believe in any specific religion then just let go to life itself.

No one can control every aspect of their life. It just IS, it just happens. We can influence things in a small way but to get obsessed with controlling everything is just a dead end. All human beings want to exert some control over what happens in their lives. Many get obsessed about it. But addicts do not have the luxury of obsession. If we obsess then we are just giving our inner Beast another source of energy.

Trying to control life is like trying to capture a specific snowflake in your hand during a blizzard. There are millions of flakes swirling down in random, unpredictable patterns. The movement of each snowflake can influence the path of another and currents of wind will send groups of flakes whirling about in incomprehensible ways. If a snowflake was self-aware could it predict how it will be influenced or where it will end up?

There is no way you can force snow to fall the way you might want it to. There is no way to predict what flake will land where. It is beyond our power and comprehension so the best thing to do is just enjoy it. Stand there and watch the intricate, beautiful dance of snow as the sunlight glistens on each crystalline surface.

We are unique individuals as each snowflake is unique. We may have some insight on how things happen in the world but most of it is beyond our comprehension. Trying to control or even fully comprehend most things is counter productive because it just creates frustration, anger, and despair. But, just allowing life to happen and enjoying it as it occurs is a beautiful way to live.

We are all part of Life. Every human being, every animal, insect, fish, tree, flower, and blade of grass is part of this. I often stand out in my back yard, plant my feet in the grass and just try to let go of my ego, my thoughts and just Be part of everything around me. Sometimes I can just be aware of existence itself, in the moment, and feel as if I am part of the entire world. I am not alone, not struggling with my one single life but part of everything. In that context, my simple problems are put into perspective.

**Spirituality is just accepting life as it comes.** Do what you can to improve your situation but just accept life. Accept your addiction totally and completely and it loses all power over you. So you can't drink or drug, so what? Can you climb every mountain? Can you fly without the aid of complicated machines?

In the "Seven Spiritual Laws of Success", Deepak Chopra elegantly expresses the following about The Law of Least Effort:

*The first thing is to accept people, situations, and events as they are, not as you wish them to be...you can intend for things to be different in the future, but in this moment, accept things as they are."*

Think how hard life can be when we don't accept it. We are always fighting life, fighting the moment.

We spend so much energy on things we cannot control in a vain attempt to comprehend. Wouldn't it be easier to just accept life as it is? Wouldn't it be simpler to just manage the things we are able to with the best of our ability and accept the results?

Accept your life, accept your addiction, that is spirituality. Stop reacting to everything that occurs in your life and just let it happen. Embrace all the good you can find, no matter how trivial it may seem at the time. Just observe rather than judge. That is the basis of a happy life for anyone, addict or non-addict.

Joe, a good friend of mine, passed out a handout one day in a meeting, listing ways of recognizing spiritual awakening.

1) An increased tendency to let things happen rather than make them happen.
2) Feelings of being connected with others and nature.
3) A tendency to think and act spontaneously rather than from past fears.
4) An unmistakable ability to enjoy each moment.
5) A loss of the ability to worry.
6) A loss of interest in conflict.
7) A loss of interest in judging others.
8) A loss of interest in judging self.
9) Gaining the ability to love without expecting anything in return.

All of those things you will find yourself embracing automatically and without effort if you follow what we have talked about in this book. Live mindfully, accept life as it comes, don't use no matter what.

# Observing your Thoughts

**Your vision will become clear only when you look into your heart... Who looks outside, dreams. Who looks inside, awakens.**
**- Carl Jung**

The human mind is a marvelous instrument, the part of us that makes us human instead of just animals. Our creativity and rational thinking come from this marvelous mind. The human mind has made us the dominant species on this planet and yet the human mind that has done so much for us also is destroying the earth as well as ourselves.

We build vast, beautiful works of architecture, compose hauntingly lovely songs, write heart wrenching poems and books, discover the secrets of the atom, and formulate the physical laws of the universe. We also pour pollutants into our water, land, and atmosphere. We abuse our bodies and minds through drugs, overeating, lack of exercise, mind numbing television. We commit genocide, destroy entire species of animals, and conduct pogroms of hatred.

Some of us have overcome obstacles all our lives by thinking through them. There has never been anything we couldn't get past if we thought enough about it. But, our addiction is proof against the power of the mind. In fact, our minds are what kept us drinking and drugging for so long. The Beast is a part of us and it can be difficult to tell who originated the thought, us or the addictive Beast.

If you practice mindful living and the other techniques that we discussed earlier then you will automatically start observing your thoughts. There are some excellent books on the subject for you to read as well. Deepak Chopra and Eckhart Tolle as well as many others explain this quite lucidly.

In "The Power of Now", Eckhart Tolle says, "The mind is a superb instrument if used rightly. Used wrongly, however, it becomes very destructive. To put it more accurately, it is not so much that you use your mind wrongly—you usually don't use it at all. It uses you."

How many of you can relate to that? Instead of using our

wonderful, rational minds we end up thinking things that are completely irrational and commit deeds we normally would not do if we gave ourselves a chance to rationally ponder a bit about it.

Our thoughts create fear, worry, anxiety, paranoia, anger, and everything else negative. We worry that we are not good enough, not wealthy enough, not strong enough. We never seem to be satisfied with our current circumstances but always yearn for more. We look to the past and either glorify it or shudder with horror. We look to the future and see either something we think is better, or the continuation of our ruin.

Our thoughts create our emotions and we are not even aware it is happening. How often do we feel down or sad and it is a result of a stray thought. One moment we'll be content and in a good mood. We think of something negative and all of a sudden we don't feel so content. We feel as if we are missing something or something "bad" is going to happen. The sun seems dimmer, the breeze cloying instead of refreshing. If we backtrack to the thought that caused our perceptions to change, suddenly we can feel good again. It is astonishing how linked our thoughts and emotions can be.

Our minds are truly powerful and we must use them appropriately. They can lift us to the greatest heights or bury us in a morass of fear and despair.

 If you are living in the current moment then everything can be ok. How else is there to live if we are to be happy? We cannot control the world in every aspect. At best we can affect tiny changes in the world. If we find ourselves in a situation that we find intolerable or even just uncomfortable then we really only can change the situation or accept it.

What does all this have to do with addiction? It has everything to do with addiction. Addiction is a physiologically triggered mental condition. Even if you are not currently using, your mind remembers and the addict in you will want to get back to a state of impairment.

The addict in you knows every button to push, every thought or emotion that will lead you back to using, based on past experiences. When you feel down, angry, afraid, or anxious, your addictive self is ready to manipulate your mind and emotions.

This is when you need to break the cycle before it gets too strong. Fighting your addiction only ends in failure because when you expend energy to battle your own self, you just end up feeding the Beast inside. You have to learn to listen to your thoughts and distinguish between the addictive self and your own, rational self.

Your addictive self is powerless without your intervention. You are the one that takes the drink or drug, all your addictive self can do is try to convince you. It is obvious now why we need to be aware of our thoughts and emotions and distinguish between self and addict-self.

Pause...focus on that space between thoughts. Call someone on the phone and tell them what you are thinking and feeling. Sit and breathe. Go outside and take a hike. Break the mental-emotional cycle. These cycles don't last long unless you obsess on them.

Watching your thoughts and emotions is vital to recovery. Even if you meditate, use CBT techniques, do journal writing, or whatever, it takes times to quiet the addictive self. If you feel angry, depressed, frustrated, or anxious just pause and examine that feeling. Why do you feel that way? What were you thinking about?

Many times it isn't a single thought stream but many disparate thoughts that work together to create the emotion. If you do not break the self-feeding cycle of negative thinking that creates negative emotions, the negative emotions will generate more negative thoughts to add to the mix. It can get quite messy and unmanageable.

So just take time, be patient with yourself. Watch your thoughts pass through your mind and ask "Is this me or my addictive self?"

However, as we've said before, you can't think your way through addiction. What you can do is learn to pay attention to your thinking, recognize the addictive voice, and modify the way you react to your thoughts and emotions. You can do self-checks to identify distorted thinking. You can use other people as sounding boards.

By taking time to observe your thoughts you can achieve a level of control over them. By living mindfully you will find yourself judging less and keeping your mind clear for pure experience.

Strive to accept life and try NOT to think it into submission. Existence is a precious and fragile thing and we can only truly succeed if we value it. An addict that is actively using values nothing.

# Meditation

*Nothing contributes so much to tranquilize the mind as a steady purpose--a point on which the soul may fix its intellectual eye.*
*- Mary Shelley*

Meditation is a mental discipline by which one attempts to get beyond reactive thinking into a deeper state of awareness. Meditation has been practiced for as long as humans have been on this planet and is a component of many religions in one form or another.

In recent decades, the Western world has become fascinated with meditation and much research has been conducted. Meditation is becoming a recommended treatment to help a wide range of physiological and psychological problems.

Meditation takes many forms including the physical, such as yoga, gardening, or simply walking. What most consider to be traditional meditation is sitting quietly. We will suggest a few ways to meditate including electronic meditation. The goal is to achieve a higher state of consciousness, a greater mental focus, enhanced creativity, a deeper self-awareness, or perhaps just a more relaxed and peaceful frame of mind.

Meditation is a valuable technique to practice. When we meditate we are letting go of our outside lives, of our thoughts and preconceptions, we are just experiencing life without expectation or judgment. Meditation brings a sense of fullness and completion. Through meditation you may experience a euphoria that far surpasses the shallow and self destructive euphoria you sought through drugs.

Meditation is an adventure of self-discovery and it can increase awareness of what is going on inside you. Following are a few meditation techniques. Find the method that suits you best or pick your own technique. If you are religious then prayer can be an excellent way to meditate. Just taking a walk or listening to music and not thinking about things is very beneficial. The key is to "let go" of your unruly, ego-focused mind and just experience life.

# Sitting

Meditating in a sitting position is popular and a part of all meditation traditions. Begin by finding a relatively quiet place to meditate where you will not be disturbed. There are many variations to this method but just sitting and breathing is the simplest.

Find a quiet room, a comfortable place outside, somewhere without many distractions. Eventually you will be able to do this anywhere but initially, find somewhere quiet and private.

You can sit on the floor with your legs crossed in front of you. You can sit in a half-lotus or lotus position. You can sit in a chair or recliner. After some practice, you can do this while lying down but right now, sit up or you'll find yourself falling asleep!

Close your eyes and consciously relax your body. Be aware of the tension in your shoulders and neck, in your back or legs. Be aware of the muscular tension in your face, at your temples. Slowly relax those muscles and mentally repeat "With each breath I relax more and more." Breathe slowly and deeply and repeat that phrase. You will feel your body relax.

Be aware of each slow breath you take. Inhale slowly through your nose and exhale slowly through your mouth. Feel the air enter your nose, expand your throat and lungs. Feel your diaphragm lower. Pause for a moment and gently release the breath through your mouth.

When thoughts arise, just be aware of them and let them go. Focus on your breath and how each breath feels as it enters and leaves you. Don't specifically try to NOT think or you'll just feed that busy mind of yours. Just be aware of your thoughts and let them go. Every time a thought comes up, re-focus on breathing. In time, you will just be sitting and breathing and you will feel very peaceful. Sit straight and try not to slump. An erect spine will ensure relaxed, full breaths and help keep you alert.

## Seizing The Moment

Another basic approach to meditation is to relax, let go, and do nothing. Don't focus on your breathing, just sit. Surrender to the moment and watch yourself, watch your thoughts. This is a technique described by many practitioners and it is easy to do once you attempt it a few times.

When thoughts come into your mind just observe them without adding to them by your active participation. Be a detached and passive observer.

Don't worry about the thoughts. It is doubtful that any of us can simply not think. Just be aware of them and let them go. Just let the thoughts come and go and sit quietly.

If you try to seize that moment of time between thoughts, as we mentioned in the preceding chapter, you can find an extraordinary moment of peace and tranquility. You can do this at any point during the day, whether you are in a busy room, walking down a sidewalk, sitting at your desk, watching your children play. It only takes a moment to slip in between thoughts and hold that space. You are still aware of everything around you but a deep calmness and tranquility can come over you because you are not judging, you are not running from thought to thought, you are just BEing.

As I mentioned previously, this is my most frequent and favorite way to give myself "no-mind" breaks throughout my day. When my mind starts whirling about without stop I just reach in between thoughts and pause for a bit. It is absolutely amazing how much good that does for me. My mind quiets, the muscles of my neck relax, my shoulders loosen. I often find myself with an involuntary smile on my face for no reason except I am just BEing instead of DOing.

## Do Anything Meditation

Just sitting and listening to music without thinking about it is meditation. Walking and just being aware of the world about you without analyzing it or thinking about it is meditation. The goal is to "get out of yourself" and give your analytic mind a break.

Sitting and watching the wind brush through the tree branches, or ruffle the surface of the water or grass is a good meditation. Just observing nature as it exists.

Gardening, splitting wood, singing, and dancing can all be forms of meditation if you do just that alone. Don't think about anything but what you are doing.

Taking a walk and just ambling along without judging or analyzing what you experience is a mindful, moving meditation. The same with gardening or mowing the yard. The key is to let your thoughts fade and just BE.

Meditate every day or even twice a day if you can. Set a routine time to do it so it becomes an integral part of your life. Ignore that rational, overly busy mind that tells you this is boring or useless.

## Focused Meditation

Focused meditation is a technique where you put yourself into a deep, relaxed, receptive state and then focus on a particular issue or just repeat affirmations. Self-hypnosis is basically focused meditation.

There are many different ways to achieve a receptive state but here is one effective technique:

1. Find a comfortable place and relax

- Find a room somewhere that is quiet and you will have privacy.
- Either lie down flat or lean back in a recliner, however you are most comfortable
- Let your arms and legs relax and not cross one another.
- Shift about until you feel comfortable. Try to have your spine straight rather than twisted to one side.

2. Physical induction

- Start taking slow, deep breaths
- As you inhale, think "With each breath..."
- As you exhale, think "...I relax more and more."
- Just be aware of breathing and after awhile your breaths will come slower and naturally. Don't try to force deep breathing, just let your body take over but stay mentally aware of each breath and continue repeating the inhale/exhale thoughts.

As you breath effortlessly, mentally focus on each part of your body, starting with your head and scalp and relax any muscles that feel tense. Continue down through your face, neck, shoulders, arms, hands, chest, stomach, hips, legs, and feet. Start at your head again and move your awareness down the back of your head through your neck and all the way down your spine.

Do this several times to completely relax. There is no hurry so feel free to do this exercise several times.

3. Mental induction

- When you are deeply relaxed you are already partially relaxed mentally.

- if your eyes are not closed, close them and just be aware of your relaxed body. When thoughts come up, just notice them and let them go.
- Become aware of each breath and
- As you inhale, think "With each breath..."
- As you exhale, think "I sink deeper and deeper."
- After a period of time your body will feel heavy and relaxed, your thoughts will come slowly.

4. Affirmations

You are ready to repeat positive affirmations. Either do this mentally or have a tape/CD running. In practice, I usually make a CD that will have 10 minutes of silence in the beginning to allow me to relax and sink into the meditative, receptive state that the first three steps accomplish. The CD then starts going through the affirmations with my not needing to do anything but sit there and listen in a dreamlike state. If you want to do it "manually", just start repeating a list of affirmations or musing about an issue that you want to focus on this session. I often have some tranquil music playing in the background or just nature sounds such as ocean waves, a stream, wind, or something similar.

5. When you are finished, start breathing slowly and deeply again, stretch your arms, legs, and back slowly. Open your eyes and feel yourself relaxed and aware and positive. This is a very powerful technique that can be used to deal with just about anything you want to work on whether it is anxiety, addictions, fear, self-consciousness, and so on. It is something you can do every day and as the days go by you will see changes in yourself. Like everything else in this book, this is not magic but a useful technique with cumulative effects.

We spent so much of our past lives programming ourselves to react in certain ways. Many of the ways are not suitable to our new clean and sober lives. Focused meditation can help re-program our behavior, our thoughts, and our emotions.

Below are two affirmations "scripts" that you might want to use or adapt. Note the use of "you" instead of "I". Referring to yourself in the 2nd person is much more effective in a focused meditation. You can easily create your own scripts. Just be sure to always be positive. Avoid using the word "not" or any other negativity. For example, instead of saying "I do not like to smoke cigarettes." it is more effective to say something like "I love the clean, pure air I breathe."

## Positiveness and Success
-You have no unnecessary fear of failure.
-You have no unnecessary anxiety.
-You find it easy to discard negative thoughts and attitudes about yourself.
-You always think of yourself in a positive way.
-You expect to succeed because you are a naturally successful person.
-You work hard to succeed and you will succeed because you deserve to succeed.
-You are tenacious and persevere with all your efforts towards success.
-You plan for success and find success.
-Your goals become closer with every day that passes.
-You move steadily towards your goals.
-You are more confident with each day that passes.
-You are a worthwhile and loveable person.
-You like yourself and deserve every good thing in life.
-You are your own person, no one controls you.
-You are forthright, trustworthy and honest.
-You face fears and responsibilities.
-You are always relaxed and assured in everything you do.
-You are enthusiastic and positive about your life.
-You look forward to change.

## CR Affirmations
-You can accept that you are less than a perfect human being.
-You do make mistakes like any other human. If you make a mistake it doesn't mean you ARE a mistake.
-Because you want a specific thing or for people to behave in specific ways doesn't mean that will happen.
-You can regret mistakes you have made, forgive yourself, learn from the mistake and choose not to blame yourself or others.
-You have a mix of qualities, skills, and experiences. Some you consider good and some not so good. None of those totally define you because you are a mix of all of them.
-Confidence is about accepting yourself as you are and accepting others as they are. It doesn't matter what happens, we are who

we are.
-You accept life as it comes.
-Acceptance is the key to living with joy and serenity.
-Acceptance is spirituality.
-The past is gone, tomorrow might not come, today is what matters.
-You are what you think. Positive thoughts lift you up, negative thoughts take you down.
-A happy, fulfilling life is something you want and will work for.
-You are responsible for yourself and for your actions.
-The more you give, the more you will receive.
-You have the power to change yourself.


Regular meditation will change your life. But, you have to do it regularly. It will take time but you will find yourself reacting less and acting more. You will find patience where you once were fidgeting. You will find compassion when before you didn't care. You will find that you can accept life on life's terms and it is OK.

Meditation is the most important activity to add to your daily schedule. You may be tempted to skip it because it doesn't feel like it is doing anything but if you do, you are depriving yourself of something critical to your recovery. In our active addiction we sought relentlessly for oblivion. Through meditation and mindfulness we can find true peace.

# Electronic Meditation

Electronic meditation, you say? How convenient! Yes, it is convenient and it really works. Mind machines have been around for decades and are utilized for a variety of purposes. The technique is called AVS, or Audio Visual Stimulation. There are many manufacturers and models to choose from but most people don't need something expensive to accomplish simple but effective meditation. These machines can be utilized for a wide variety of purposes such as relaxation, sleep aids, release of pain, behavior modification, increased concentration and learning, and so on.

They are not very expensive and are simple to use. If you are new to using mind machines look for something by MindPlace such as the Proteus or Procyon. Mind-Gear also has good machines as well as Photosonix and other companies. The Cognitive Recovery website at http://cognitiverecovery.net has recommended machines and links.

A mind machine uses pulsing rhythmic sound usually with a flashing light to alter the brainwave frequency of the user. Mind machines can induce deep states of relaxation, concentration and, in some cases, altered states of consciousness that are often compared with those obtained from deep meditation. The process is known as entrainment. The combination of sound and light actually entrains the brain (suggests to it) to adopt a different rhythm.

Meditation can encourage a user to reach deep levels but that often takes decades of practice. A mind machine gets you there fast. Is it the same quality though? That is up for argument but if a machine can help teach you to reach deep states of awareness quickly, it can't be all bad. We are all for the benefits of a committed program in meditation and this should not be neglected but it can be very helpful to reach deep, relaxed states quickly as well.

A typical mind machine will consist of the actual machine that generates audio and visual patterns, a pair of headphones, and goggles that contain LED lights. When a specific program contains binaural beats, the effect is generally much more effective.

Binaural beats may very well influence functions of the brain besides those related to hearing. This is called a frequency following response. The concept is that if one receives a stimulus with a frequency in the range of brain waves, the predominant brain wave frequency is likely to move towards the frequency of the stimulus. This is the entrainment that we mentioned before. In addition, binaural beats seem to relate to both spatial perception and stereo auditory recognition, and even activation of different areas of the brain. Binaural beats are said to lead to increased learning and creativity.

The power of mind machines is that they get you out of your own mind quickly, away from constant thinking. It gives you a break and can teach you to relax and let go. If you relax and just enjoy the lights and sounds then you are not thinking and that by itself is a benefit. The more often you can find times to relax deeply and not think so much, the better off you are.

If you utilize such a machine and can reach a deep, relaxed state of awareness easily, it is a perfect environment to boost your psychological defenses against the addictive self by repeating positive affirmations. It is a highly effective supplemental method to help re-program some of the unhelpful behaviors you developed in your using years.

As time goes on, expect to find mind machines utilized in therapeutic environments more commonly. With a client in a relaxed, receptive state, therapy can be much easier and more effective.

That should be enough information to convince you that a mind machine could be another useful tool for your sobriety toolbox. They are useful for quick breaks during the day that relax, or energizing creativity as well as deeper meditational states. They are excellent sleep aids as well if you need that.

# Relaxation Techniques

So often we find ourselves tensed up and stressed out. That is a way of life for a lot of people from the moment they get out of bed in the morning until they fall back into it that night. Not only does this keep us on edge all day but we cannot function efficiently or live mindfully if we are under physical tension continually.

It can be tough staying clean and sober when you are on edge all the time. If you are practicing mindful living and meditation, you probably are more relaxed than you used to be but there are often times it is very helpful to purposely let go and relax physically.

There are many physical meditations such as yoga, qigong, tai chi, and so on that help you relax and are beneficial in many ways but just intentionally relaxing your body can be enormously beneficial.

## Progressive relaxation.

Lie down somewhere comfortable or even just sit back in a comfortable position.

The basic process is to tense an area and then completely relax it.

Start with your right foot and ankle. Curl your toes, spread your toes, pull your foot back and forward, tense it and then just let it relax.

Tense your right lower leg and then relax.

Tense your entire right leg and then let it relax.

Do the same to your left leg.

Move to your right hand and forearm. Tense and relax.

Then the entire right arm, tense it and relax.

Do the same to your left arm.

Tighten your abdomen and relax.

Tighten and flex your chest...and relax.

Tense/relax your shoulders and neck.

Tense your entire face and head, grit your teeth, screw your eyes shut and open them wide...and then relax it all.

## Awareness relaxation

As before, lie or sit comfortably.

Close your eyes and try to just be aware of your body. Start at the very crown of your head and be aware of any tension in your scalp, around your eyes, in your jaw, at the back of your neck. As you mentally visit each area just relax every muscle.

Visit the neck again and relax.

Move to your shoulders and relax them.

Proceed one by one through your arms and hands, your chest, abdomen, hips, lower back, legs and feet.

Once you reach your toes...do the whole process again to verify and you'll often find something tensed up again somewhere in the process. A lot of people tense their jaws, the skin of their face or forehead, the neck or lower back.

This can be a pretty rapid process so don't be shy about doing it several times.

Then just sit or lie there completely relaxed.

This technique can be used anywhere, whether riding the bus, sitting on the ground, or sitting at your desk.

Those two are basic techniques that anyone can become proficient with easily. There are lots of books and sites on the internet that contain more relaxation techniques.

# Closing Thoughts

**We are what we repeatedly do. Excellence, therefore, is not an act but a habit.**
**- Aristotle**

Use positive self-talk and be proud that you are not engaging in harmful behaviors anymore. Set up a morning/evening ritual for yourself to reaffirm your intent, what you want out of life. Use affirmations, read inspirational books, listen to relaxing music, meditate, pray, whatever you need to do to let go of day to day life for awhile and just be yourself. In the appendices are some affirmations that you might use.

If we want to live in fear, we will do that. If we want to live in sadness, we can certainly do that as well. If we want to live with active addictions, that will definitely happen. But, we don't have to!

What do you want from life? What do you want from yourself? Make lists of pros and cons about your lifestyle. Look at your behavior, how you react to life, how you live now and how you want to live. Study these lists and determine what your life will be. Hold that in your mind as much as you can at all times and you will have that life.

Focus on living mindfully and working with others. By helping others you indeed help yourself. Get involved in life. See where you can help out in your community. Keep alert to the voice of your Beast and utilize the cognitive techniques we have discussed in this book to examine your thoughts and emotions. Know that you can not only achieve sobriety but you can remain that way and it is not difficult to do at all. It just requires attention, awareness, and love.

Know that you are a precious human being who can live life as it comes, who can appreciate the beauty of the world and everything in it, who can change your own life to whatever you want. It will take work though, nothing comes without effort. But every iota of effort you put into recovery will be rewarded a thousand times over.

# Appendices

## Recovery Groups

**AA and NA** - Just open your phone book or go to www.google.com to find out all you want to know about 12-step groups. You can almost always find a 12-step meeting to attend. The official AA site is at http://www.aa.org/.

There are a lot of secular recovery groups as well. They are not widespread yet but attendance and popularity are increasing.

**S.M.A.R.T.**
Founded on the principles of REBT, you can find an enormous amount of information at http://www.smartrecovery.org/. SMART is an excellent and thorough program.

**LifeRing** – A secular recovery group with a very active online forum and lots of information. http://www.unhooked.com/

**Rational Recovery** – http://rational.org/. A "recovery" program that claims to destroy (cure?) addiction. Regardless, the AVRT technique of RR is a quite valuable and very useful concept.

**S.O.S.** - A secular recovery group.
http://www.sosrecovery.org/whoweare.html

**Women For Sobriety** – A recovery group with a focus on women in recovery. http://www.womenforsobriety.org/

Information and history about 12-step groups can be found in many places. The internet is full of sites and there are many books including, of course, The Big Book. Here are a couple good web sites for historical information:

AA history by one who was there:
http://alcoholism.about.com/cs/history/a/blmitch.htm

A vast site with AA documentation, scans of old documents, history, and so on. Note that this site is rather confrontational but still possesses a lot of good info.
http://www.orange-papers.org/

# Cognitive Recovery Meetings

*Shared joy is a double joy; shared sorrow is half sorrow.*
*- Swedish proverb*

The CR meeting format is quite flexible. Each meeting usually lasts an hour. We often just talk about our week or day, share what is going on in our lives, or bring up topics that might be affecting our serenity and sobriety.

In practice, larger meetings should be discussion meetings. As people form friendships, smaller meetings can often result which are ideal for "check-in" type meetings.

Each meeting can decide if they want to allow cross-talk or refrain from it. Allowing others to comment on what another says can be very valuable but usually only works well with smaller, more intimate groups where everyone knows each other well. Cross-talk in larger meetings or with people you don't know very well can be easily misunderstood. It can be perceived as judging or "know-it-all'ing". Cross-talk is extremely helpful in small groups of people who know each other so don't disregard it. But, for larger, open meetings, it is best to avoid it.

Typically, the "chair" for the meeting is someone who volunteered to do it at the last meeting.

Whoever is chairing the meeting calls the meeting to order and reads something similar to the following:

**Hi, I'm _____.**
(if you want to label yourself an addict/alcoholic/sobrietist/whatever, feel free to do so. It is totally optional.)

**Welcome to Cognitive Recovery. We are a peer support group with a focus on addiction recovery. CR is not allied with any organization or institution. Our only purpose is to recover from addiction.**

**The problem is our thinking. Through cognitive awareness we learn to identify and change the thoughts and behaviors that make our lives less than they could be.**

We are here to share our experiences, thoughts, and feelings. We do not tell people what to do to get and stay clean and sober but may offer suggestions as we share our own experiences. The choice to be clean and sober is yours because you are the only one with the power to make that choice. We are all here to celebrate our sobriety and to support one another in sober living.

**Does anyone have any announcements?**

If the group is renting space from an organization of some type, then a basket can be passed for donations. Often probation officers or IOP treatments will require their clients to attend meetings of some type and bring back attendance slips. Those should be signed at the end of the meeting.

If donations are accepted:

**I'm passing the basket for voluntary donations that will be used only to support this group. If you have any slips to be signed, they will be signed after the meeting.**

**(start the basket around)**

**(ask for a volunteer to chair the next meeting)**

**Does anyone have a topic they would like to bring up?**

If no one supplies a topic, the chair for this meeting should be prepared to provide one or start off with their own check-in, depending on the meeting type.

There is no special way to end a meeting. Each specific meeting group is welcome to come up with their own way to finish. Read a poem or simply thank everyone for attending the meeting. I like just saying, **"Thank you for being here and helping me to stay sober and clean."**

 In fact, the suggested format is just that, a suggestion. Feel free to come up with your own meeting format.

CR meetings are informal and each individual should say what is in their heart, not just what they think they should say. Each individual should focus on the person talking and really listen to them rather than focusing on what they want to say. It is amazing how much one can gain from a meeting if you keep yourself open to another's words. Meetings can be a cheap group therapy session and extraordinarily effective. If you are open and honest and express what is going on inside of you, you help not only yourself but many others.

It is especially helpful to talk about how you have been thinking or feeling. Becoming aware of how you think and feel is vitally important. Recognizing the voice of the Beast is important. Sharing ways to live mindfully is important.

Joining with others that have the same problem as you have is a powerful thing. You learn, you teach, you feel comforted, and you belong.

Recovery meetings are one of the more important facets of getting and staying clean and sober.

There are even online meetings on the internet either via online forums or in real-time chat sessions. Those can be extraordinarily useful for those of us around computers a lot. Internet forums are there 24/7/365 and if you find an active group, you can make friends, gain support, and help others.

# Meetings, Mentors, and Therapy

CR does not have a specific "sponsor" scheme as 12-step groups do but recognizes the value of having someone with a significant amount of sober time acting as a mentor to someone new to sobriety.

An CR mentor suggests, encourages, and usually just functions as a sounding board. Deep friendships can develop between people in recovery and it makes it much easier to be completely open and honest with someone you are close to rather than someone you've just seen in a few meetings.

This is entirely optional from both sides but not only can it be very helpful to have someone guide you, it also helps the person who is mentoring you! Why does it help the other person? Because they are giving of themselves to you, they are focusing on you, they are getting out of their own heads and doing something helpful for another individual, someone who is suffering from the same disease they have. That is an enormous benefit.

A mentor will suggest books to read, meetings to attend, CBT or other techniques to practice. A mentor may not always agree with you or have the answer you want, but will listen to you.

Get as many phone numbers from other members as you can and be sure to keep in touch. It helps a lot to just talk to another addict. Identify two or three that you can call at absolutely any time, in an emergency. It can be a lifesaver to know you have someone you can call at 3am in the morning if you really have to.

How many meetings do you need to attend? You are the only one that can judge that. Many people go to as many meetings as they can, especially in the beginning, while others will go to very few. Meetings help keep you centered, focused, and accountable.

Most often people will go to a lot of meetings at first and gradually go to less as time goes by. Just don't get complacent and think you can do it by yourself! If you start noticing uncomfortable feelings then it is probably time to find some fellow addicts and get together.

Group therapy sessions or private therapy is also highly recommended, especially at first. After abusing a substance for so long, our way of thinking is quite dysfunctional and we have a lot to unlearn. Utilize every resource you can find.

With any luck you will encounter a caring, experienced addiction therapist who can conduct an effective motivational interview with you and help you see where you need to change. Remember that YOU have to make the change but another person can be invaluable in helping you see clearly.

There are usually IOP (Intensive Out Patient) groups you can sign up for as well as other resources. It may seem uncomfortable at first, sitting in a group and talking to others but that is one of the best ways to learn about your own self. A good therapist who can listen and lead the group smoothly is invaluable.

# CBT Worksheets

There are many CBT/REBT worksheets on the internet that can be viewed/downloaded. Here are a few sites:

- http://www.smartrecovery.org/resources/toolchest.htm
- http://www.martincbt.com/handouts.html
- http://www.livingcbt.com/freeselfhelp.html
- http://www.specialtybehavioralhealth.com/pdfs-cognitive-behavioral-therapy

Highly recommended are the resources at www.smartrecovery.org. The worksheets they make freely available for download cover a wide range and are very useful.

You can also make an excellent worksheets from the following pages by copying/printing them or just download the worksheets from http://www.cognitiverecovery.net.

# Daily Reflection (What happened today?)

**Situation.** Write down what happened

**Thoughts/Emotions.** Describe what you were thinking and feeling.

**Emotional Level.** How intensely were you feeling?

**Alternate (helpful) Thoughts/Emotions.** What else could you have thought about a situation and how would you have felt?

**New Emotional Level.** How intensely were you feeling after applying alternate thoughts and feelings?

**Date** _____

**Weekly Diary** (What happened this week?)
Keep your Daily Reflection worksheets for a week and review them.




**Monthly Diary** (What happened this month?)
Keep your Daily Reflection worksheets for a month and review them. Do you see a change?


Feel free to hold onto your monthly diary collection for six months, a year, or more so you can go back and review things. This isn't like a normal daily diary but a daily check that you simply accumulate as the days go by. It can be very valuable when you look back over the last month or several and actually see changes you are making.

# Distorted Thinking Checklist
(Are you doing any of these? Carry this list in your wallet!)

**All or Nothing Thinking**

**Mental Filtering**

**Disqualifying the Positive**

**Mind Reading**

**Fortune Telling**

**Catastrophizing**

**Labeling/Mislabeling**

**Magnifying or Minimizing**

**Emotional Reasoning**

**Shoulds**

**Over Generalizing**

**Personalization**

**Compensatory Misconceptions**

# Attitudes and Behavior Checklist

- If I have tried and failed, can I use what I have learned?

- Am I realistic about my abilities and limitations?

- Am I willing to admit there is room for improvement in my relationships with my family and friends?

- Can I take a stand and express my opinions diplomatically?

- Have I truly accepted addiction as a mental illness?

- Have I learned that no matter what events may occur, no matter what other people may do, I can always choose my attitude?

- Am I wise enough not to expect a partner not to fill all my emotional needs?

- Do I accept responsibility to do something about my problems as they arise?

- Do I set my goals realistically?

- Can I relax when I am by myself?

- Have I kept an open mind, willing to learn no matter what?

- Can I apologize when I'm wrong?

- Do I treat myself well physically, mentally, and spiritually?

- Do I associate with emotionally healthy people?

- Do I enjoy my own company?

- Do I realize that a healthy form of self-love is needed in my relationships with others?

- Am I consistent in my loving attitude toward my friends and family?

- Am I open and honest in my relationships?

- Do I know the difference between detachment and indifference?

- Have I let go of the people and situations I cannot change?

- Do I let others know the real me?

- Have I developed a tolerant, easy-going attitude toward myself?

- Am I tolerant of others?

- Do I expect others to make special allowances for my behavior?

- Am I able to say no?

- Are my responsibilities to myself kept in good balance with my desire to reach out to others?

- Do I make an effort to consider the needs of others as well as my own?

- Can I compromise realistically?

- Do I avoid judging others?

- Have I eliminated the shoulds and oughts from my vocabulary?

- Do I respect the feelings and experience of others?

- Have I developed some sense of my right to be treated with dignity?

- Do I have patience with myself?

- Can I patiently teach others what I have learned, appreciating their willingness to learn?

- Can I be accommodating and still maintain my self-respect?

- Do I understand that reality is what is happening, not what I think or feel is happening?

- Do I make my own decisions?

- Do I try to understand another's position, even though I may not agree with it?

- Am I comfortable in my social interactions with others?

- Once a conflict is over and I have expressed my anger, can I let go?

- Can I avoid blaming others and accept responsibility for my own actions?

- Do I look for the best in each situation and person that I encounter?

- Do I recover quickly from disappointment?

- Do I listen attentively when others are talking or am I just waiting my turn to speak?

- Do I know the difference between asking for help and imposing?

- Do I treat others kindly, considering their feelings?

- Do I see value in simply lending a listening ear to someone in need?

- Can I accept the love that others offer to me?

- Am I conscientious and tactful in my interactions with

others, always considering their feelings?

- Are my feelings expressed in appropriate ways?

- Do I try to say what I mean and mean what I say?

- Do I do what I have promised to do?

- Do I avoid rationalizing or justifying my faults?

- Can I be completely honest, not lying to myself or others?

- Can I admit to others and myself when I am wrong?

- Do I know that a humbling experience is not a humiliating one?

- Can I share another's problems without worrying about them?

- Do I see value in talking to someone about my fears?

- Am I willing to focus on living in the present, in the moment?

- Do I realize that willingness to do something is the first step to actually doing it?

- Do I realize that procrastination often leads to justification for missed opportunities?

- Do I have a purpose in my life?

- Can I discipline myself in a healthy and comfortable way so that I can accomplish things?

- Do I avoid feeling responsible for others lives, but see myself as having responsibilities to others?

- Do I appreciate my talents and abilities?


Date _____

# Affirmations to read every morning and evening.

I can accept that I am a less than perfect human being. I do make mistakes like any other human. If I make a mistake it doesn't mean I AM a mistake.

Because I want a specific thing or for people to behave in specific ways doesn't mean that will happen.

I can regret mistakes I have made, forgive myself, learn from the mistake and choose not to blame myself or others.

I have a mix of qualities, skills, and experiences. Some I consider good and some not so good. None of those totally define me because I am a mix of all of them.

Confidence is about accepting myself as I am and accepting others as they are.

I accept life as it comes. Acceptance is the key to living with joy and serenity.

The past is gone, tomorrow might not come, today is what matters.

I am what I think. Positive thoughts lift me up, negative thoughts take me down.

A happy, fulfilling life is something I want and will work for.

I am responsible for myself and for my actions.

The more I give, the more I will receive.

I have the power to change myself.

# Daily Schedule

This is something you need to create for yourself but here are some basics to start with.

Give yourself quiet time in the morning and evening of every day to reflect on your sobriety and to just BE. Try not to think, daydream, or plan during these times, just exist. Be grateful and positive.

Take frequent opportunities during the day to pause between thoughts and just relax. Focus on the Moment and feel happiness, calmness, and optimism flow into you.

Be aware of your thoughts and emotions.

Be aware of your addictive voice.

Take an opportunity every day to talk to someone. Be grateful that you are alive. Be grateful that you are sober. Gratitude is an amazing emotion that can make every day worthwhile.

Remember that each day is an opportunity to learn and to grow. Don't waste it.

Utilize self-checks throughout the day and spend time each evening looking back over the day to see where you may have done better.

Don't Use, No Matter What!

Appreciate your life, your friends, and family. We never know what tomorrow will bring so tell someone you love them each day, even if that person is just yourself.

# Reading Material

Here are a few books that are enlightening, thought provoking, and helpful to a person in recovery. One good way to find books that appeal to you personally is to go to the Google search engine on the web and search for a topic, such as "CBT books", "meditation", or whatever and then go to Amazon or another bookstore site and read reviews and such about that book. An even better way is talk to other people and find out what they are reading! There is a wealth of reading material out there that is helpful!

**HH Dalai Lama and Howard C. Cutler**
-The Art of Happiness

**Al J. Mooney**
**Arlene Eisenberg**
**Howard Eisenberg**
-The Recovery Book

**Melody Beattie**
-The Language of Letting Go

**Richard Carlson**
-Don't Sweat The Small Stuff (and it's all small stuff)

**Deepak Chopra**
-Seven Spiritual Laws of Success
-Freedom From Addiction

**Thich Nhat Hanh**
-Peace Is Every Step

**Don Miguel Ruiz**
-The Four Agreements.

**Hayes/ Strosahl/ Wilson**
-Acceptance and Commitment Therapy: An Experiential Approach to Behavior Change

**Ernest Kurtz and Katherine Ketchum**
-The Spirituality of Imperfection

**LifeRing Press**
-Keepers , Voices of Secular Recovery

**Rian McMullin**
-The New Handbook of Cognitive Therapy Techniques

**Martin Nicholas**
- Recovery By Choice

**Eckhart Tolle**
-The Power of Now

**McKay, Wood, Brantley**
-Dialectical Behavior Therapy Skills Workbook

**Marsha M. Linehan**
-Skills Training Manual for Treating Borderline Personality Disorder

**James A. Milam/Katherine Ketcham**
-Under the Influence

## Useful Internet Sites

There are hundreds of excellent sites out there dealing with CBT, recovery, meditation, and other topics that are immensely useful. Just go to http://www.google.com and start searching! Besides the sites mentioned earlier in the Appendices, the following are also useful:

**NIMH, National Institute of Mental Health**
http://www.nimh.nih.gov

**National Association of Cognitive Behavioral Therapists**
http://www.nacbt.org

**Behavioral Tech, LLC**
http://behavioraltech.org/

# A Creed to Live By

Don't undermine your worth by comparing yourself with others,

It is because we are different that each of us is special.

Don't set your goals by what other people deem important,

Only you know what is best for you.

Don't take for granted the things closest to your heart

Cling to that as you would your life, for without them life is meaningless.

Don't let your life slip through your fingers by living in the past or the future.

Don't give up when you still have something to give

Nothing is really over ... until the moment you stop trying.

Don't be afraid to admit that you are less than perfect, It is the fragile thread that binds us to each other.

Don't be afraid to encounter risks. It is by taking chances that we learn how to be brave.

Don't shut love out of your life by saying it's impossible to find.

The quickest way to receive love is to give love.

Don't dismiss your Dreams. To be without dreams is to be without hope. To be without hope is to be without purpose.

Life is not a race, but a journey to be savored every step of the way.

**May your life be sober and fulfilling.**
**You are the only one who can create that life and you CAN do it.**